Emotions Simplified: A Practical Self-Help Workbook

A 5-Part Holistic Approach to Unlocking Your Best Potential

Glenda D. Quinto

Alchemy Publishing Group, LLC
Reidsville, NC 27320
888-870-2519
www.alchemy-publishing.com
Managing Editor - Juliana A. Inhofer

ISBN: 978-1-63297-009-1
First Edition
Published in the United States of America
All Rights Reserved

Table of Contents

Introduction

Metaphorically, if your life is a puzzle, why is it that you can't seem to put some or all of the puzzle pieces where they belong? Why is it that although your life is uncomfortable in some way, you continue to ignore your feelings and emotions rather than deal with them? How can you feel comfortable, confident and in charge of your life, when the world around you feels uncertain?

The goal of this workbook is to help you regain control of your life by understanding your current state of emotional well-being and to provide you with a clear roadmap to reach your life goals. By taking this 5-part holistic approach, you will gain a well-balanced awareness of your emotional health and you can begin to determine your individual path that will lead to unlocking your best potential.

I remember being a young child and experiencing something fundamentally wrong with my parents' behavior and wondering "How is it that I could see it and they cannot?" Somehow, that was a defining moment in my young life when I realized I had to learn to behave as an adult to help my parents raise my younger brothers.

1

Unfortunately, when you are a child, and you are a product of a dysfunctional environment, other people treat you very differently. Even though you are, "the child" and you have nothing to do with your parents' choices, people condemn you before you have a chance to explain that their choices are not yours but rather you were born into this family and now you have to figure out a way to shape your own life.

However, it was not easy to break away from the weight of the emotional burden that stems from my parent's problems with substance abuse and their inability to grow up and become the individuals they wished they could have been. There were times I wished for someone to take the pain and fear away from me and tell me I was going to be okay, but there was no one to turn to. Our extended family was too busy criticizing my parents to think or care for a moment what that environment was doing to us as children.

Later in life I saw a couple of therapists and counselors, but I knew I was not going to find the answers I needed in just a couple of sessions. After all I didn't accumulate all these feelings overnight.

Then as I got older I began to read books to help me figure out how to get out of the turmoil I was in, and slowly I began to find answers. Through trial and error and constantly questioning my choices and decisions, I have arrived at this stage in my life, where I not only like who I am, but I have finally found as much respect and love for myself as I have always had for others.

Although, I did not know how to go about reaching my dreams, I began to realize what I did not want in my life by a process of elimination. Once I was able to recognize the traits and ideals I did not want, I began to fill my mind with traits and ideals I wanted to incorporate in my life.

My struggles at an early age served as an inspiration to pursue helping others to cut through the confusion in their lives and regain clarity. My processes have served as an invaluable lesson and have carried me into my professional adult life. By using my own experiences along with my schooling and the help I have given to others along the way, I have developed this workbook in an effort to offer readers the ability to see things in a whole new light.

Most self-help books look at only one area of your life. By using a holistic approach, looking at self, family, friends, love partners, and work, this workbook will help you recognize the traits and ideals you want to incorporate into your life. I have put together a compilation of ideas, thoughts, questions, scales, and definitions to help you figure out in a simple way how you feel about yourself as well as everyone who means something to you. I believe we always have a choice, even when we think we do not.

This workbook can help you as much as you would like or as little as you would like, it all depends on what you want out of it. It allows you to think about your life in new more in-depth ways and allows you to see where you are at in this stage of your life.

There are three ways in which to approach this workbook:

1. *You can simply read the book and use the book as a reference for whenever you need to get some answers.*

2. *You can read the book and using paper and a pencil, just work on the Scales.*

3. *You can take your time, and using paper and a pencil, go through every single question and allow yourself to open up in ways you may have never experimented with before.*

The scales are a great way to gauge how you are feeling about a particular situation in your life at any given moment. It will also help you see where your strengths lie and where there is room for growth. You may find that your numbers on the scales are great and strong when it comes to family and friends, but how you feel about yourself is affecting your love-partner relationships, as well as your ability to find a fulfilling career. The more aware you are of yourself, the better results you are going to get to begin your self-empowerment.

I have included questions in each chapter that pertain to how you perceive yourself, your family, your friends, a love-partner, and your work. You could even sit with individuals that you trust and wish to familiarize yourself with, as these questions will help you find out who they are, and they will find out who you are.

This is your life and the more you are aware of yourself, the better you can manage it. By gaining insight into your emotions and how they mold and shape every area of your life, you will have a better understanding of who you are, what you are doing right, and what to focus on changing. I am hoping you can take something with you from this workbook that will bring you some kind of solace and understanding of your life.

In this book, we will explore the many facets of ourselves and how our emotions and the decisions that we make in our daily lives can consciously or unconsciously influence how we feel about ourselves, how we treat others, and how content we can be. The most important relationship we can ever have is with ourselves. This determines our relationship with all of the people in our lives.

The way we perceive ourselves will influence so many aspects of our lives:
- Our relationship with our families
- The friends we attract
- Whether the people around us are supportive and honest, or whether they'll only tell us what we want to hear
- The type of love partner we will pick—a giver or a taker
- The job we choose—one that fulfills us, or one that just helps us pay for a roof over our heads
- Our perception of the world—as a hostile place or as a place where people come together to help each other

Before we dive into these areas, let's briefly examine each one.

Self

As individuals, we are always seeking meaning in our lives and trying to find our place in this world. When looking for answers, sometimes we embark on different journeys. This feeling of exploration can only happen when we decide to take that leap and choose to test uncharted waters; only then we can be sure of our decisions and our choices. For example, if we wanted to go on a quest of faith, we may want to seek out a different belief system than the one we were brought up with and see if it resonates with us.

Do we treat ourselves with kindness and respect, or do we judge ourselves harshly for the mistakes we make? Do we feel worthy of making our contributions in this life, or do we feel that we do not have anything to

4

offer?

Whether we are aware of it or not, our feelings dictate how we move through our day and, depending on how we see ourselves, our feelings are what determine not only how we see the world but also how we treat others around us.

Family and friends

Our family and friends play a big part in our lives. After all, they are our first teachers. Some of us enjoy and cherish the relationships we have with our friends and family. We feel as if we are always growing and learning together, sharing new ideas, and implementing those ideas into our lives, improving not only our own lives but also the lives of those around us.

Some of us may be proud of our upbringing, but along the way we feel that we've outgrown our family's beliefs. We feel that we want more out of life or that we want to seek something different that is not available from where we came. It's not that our family values are wrong, but rather that they don't fit in our quest to evolve and grow. We are seekers of a different reality, one that challenges our core being in a synergistic way and fulfills our dreams.

Love partner

Our love partner is someone we have chosen to share our multidimensional selves and experiences with. Some believe in the notion that this person will hold the key not only to our hearts but also, if we are lucky, to our hopes and dreams. When we feel understood and feel that we understand our partner, life is easier. It contains a flow that is effortless. We have the ability to focus on important aspects of our lives. This is a synergy that human beings seek in their life journey—and it can be expanded with a love partner.

Work

There are those in life who are lucky enough at a very young age to know exactly who they are and what they want to be. Individuals want to strive toward careers where they find fulfillment. Finding out our likes and dislikes is the first step toward finding a career where fulfillment and growth are possible. We may not find that dream job right away, but with a desire to seek it and through trial and error, every goal can be accomplished.

Putting it all together in life

Some of us have never experienced real support or understanding from family, from a love partner, from fellow employees at work, or from friends. All we know is that our reality is not a place where we think we can prosper and be happy. We might feel that in order to find true happiness we'll have to embark on a quest to find out what we want in life and what life we want to live, even if it means going against all that we know and all that we were taught. Some of us find ourselves trying to make sense of our past and understand how the decisions we made continue to affect our present choices. And some of us simply choose to ignore what has happened and hope our problems will just go away.

It can sometimes take a long time before any realization of these deeper emotions and anxieties manifest into actual epiphanies or calls to action. Many of us are bored with or tired of our present situation, and all we think about is a different future, one we can control and enjoy much more than the one we are in right now. Some of us really like our present life. We love our partner, our work, our family, and our friends, and all that we're looking for is a way to grow and expand within the realm of our lives and to live life to the fullest.

Most of us fall into one of three groups:

1.   *Those who have accepted their beliefs and are committed to them.* These individuals are in synergy with their minds and souls. Life can still be challenging, but at least there is understanding behind their actions.

2.   *Those who have accepted their beliefs but are in conflict.* These individuals live an exhausting life, always wondering and questioning themselves and their choices.

3.   *Those who walk around not even realizing why their lives are so difficult and why nobody understands them—including themselves.* This cognitive and emotional dissonance will eventually drive these issues to the forefront.

This book is about you, me, us, and everyone you know and will meet. To understand the idea of this book, we must begin with the *self* and what drives us to make the decisions we make.

Metaphorically, our mind and soul is our first house, where there are many rooms. Each "room" represents a part of us that we engage with daily. Like our actual living room, kitchen, and dining room, some of these rooms give us a sense of comfort and understanding. We are able to navigate them without pain or acknowledgement but rather instinctively. Each room has a use and function, whether practical, aesthetic, nostalgic, or something else entirely. There are specific rooms in our house that make us uncomfortable; these are full of feelings we choose not to acknowledge, like painful memories we wish to forget. We keep these particular rooms under lock and key. Now and then, people will compel us to walk into these rooms. They are dark but familiar, and in them lie important pieces of our "self" puzzle. If we have the courage to put those pieces together, we can shine light in those dark rooms that belong to our soul, just as much as any other, and that are waiting for us to have the courage to open and allow the light and truth to enter and set us free.

Part 1 - Self

Our feelings begin to flourish the moment we are born. Our first interaction with our parents and the way they welcome us into this world substantially helps shape or hinder our emotional nature. Although we have our own individual personality from the moment we are born, we will have to adhere to the way we are being raised until we are old enough to choose otherwise.

In our formative years, we learn their language, faith, traits, fears, and beliefs; there are good and positive influences as well as negative and harmful ones, and depending on how we perceive life, we will decide what traits will be more fitting to our personality and our way of life. As we continue to listen to our parents and watch and learn from their behavior, we form our own ways of interpreting their actions. As we grow, our family shares the traditions passed down by parents and grandparents and the generations before them. Our parents also share their new ideas that they feel might help us along the way.

When we finally reach adolescence, we begin to develop a broader spectrum of emotions, and with the help of our awakening hormones, we begin to react and respond to situations in a deeper way. Whether we are aware of it or not, our feelings start to oscillate—for example, from hating the way we look to having self-confidence and feeling all grown up. One minute we are enjoying our environment, especially when things are going our way. The next minute we are loathing every other aspect of our lives. Some individuals have loving, supportive parents who understand what their teenagers are going through and manage to teach them about the consequences of their actions. These fortunate youths are better able to feel loved and protected while going through these monumental life changes that ultimately will shape who they are.

Some, unfortunately, do not have this support. Those who do not receive such support can feel abandoned and are more prone to retaliate—not liking who their parents are, their social class, where they come from, and their place within their peer group. As teenagers, they may feel disconnected from their parents, while seeing at the same time how other teenagers do have supportive parents, wondering why they do not.

Remember, at the beginning in the introduction, I mentioned that the mind and soul are like your house where we compartmentalize our emotions into rooms where we can deal with issues depending what they are and in what part of the house we choose to put them. The positive ones, where we are happy to exhibit our joyful emotions, we put in the rooms like our living room, kitchen, and common areas where we want our friends and family to see we are doing well. However, the negative ones we want to stow away into rooms like the attic, bedrooms, closets—anywhere where they are not visible to friends and family, but most importantly, where they are not visible to us and beyond dealing with.

Positive perceptions
- Feelings of self-acceptance
- The ability to be honest with yourself
- The power to embrace life's challenges with confidence and clarity
- Pride in who you are and what you do
- The ability to nurture your body
- The ability to honor yourself by always protecting and loving yourself
- Self-forgiveness, knowing you can do better the next time you encounter a situation

Negative perceptions

- Feelings of dislike for who you are
- Uncertainty
- Lack of worthiness
- Shame for past mistakes
- Constant comparing of yourself to others, furthering guilt and feelings of worthlessness
- Self-loathing
- Putting blame on others, because you are unable to see where you went wrong

Some individuals find themselves shifting from one side of these feelings to the other. At different times in their lives, they will feel amazing and self-confident, while at other times, they will gravitate toward the more negative side of the spectrum. The question is, what can we do to feel good all the time? How can we stay grounded, happy, and secure regardless of how high or low the pendulum swings? Essentially, we need to find a way to feel proud of who we are and the role we play in this world. We need to recognize: *As we mature, the only person that can help us grow and change into who we want to be is ourselves.* No one else can help us find feelings of self-worth and self-love.

When we are not sure about our decisions or where we are heading, we begin to question whether we should do what feels right in our hearts or do what our mind thinks we should be doing. At this point, our mind and soul are in conflict, and all these feelings start to create enormous confusion. Should I do the right thing or do what I want to do, even though I know in my heart it is not a good idea? Should I pursue what my talents are and what I am good at, or should I just try and make money? Should I follow my heart's desires, or should I do what others expect me to do? Do I date someone who inspires me to be better every day, or do I date someone who is of the right social class or can take me to a higher social tier? Do I allow my family to sway me toward what they think I should be doing, or do I follow my inner compass? Do I love and support my family without trying to change their beliefs and way of life? Can I allow my family in my life without them interfering with what is best for me? Do I allow my friends to influence my decisions, or do I make my own choices? Do my friends have my best interest at heart? Can I rely on them, or do I feel used? Am I enjoying my time at work, or do I feel suffocated? Do I feel respected at my job, or do I need to move somewhere else where my expertise and talents are appreciated? Our flow of consciousness is besieged with these kinds of questions and expectations.

Every situation allows us to make the right decision for ourselves, if we are attuned to our feelings. When we find our mind and soul in conflict about any decision, this is the perfect opportunity to grow and embrace those fearful, uncertain feelings. These obstacles allow us to figure out a way to overcome our difficulties and find a resolution. The more attached we are to certain beliefs, the harder this task will be. However, overcoming such problems will empower us with a sense of understanding and knowledge we would have never experienced before. This newfound maturity will enrich our mind and soul with a sense of personal accomplishment.

Every time we come across a situation, we have numerous choices of how to go about dealing with the problem. For example: We are on the phone with a customer service representative, and we are trying to get them to not only understand our problem but also offer the solution. However, after spending what feels like hours on the phone, they haven't been able to fix the problem. You can either get frustrated and make it personal and then walk away by leaving the problem exactly as it is for another day and achieve nothing or you could go into the conversation with one goal in mind: and that is to get your problem fixed, one way or another. So your choices on how it is going to go depend on how you begin the conversation.

Positive vibrations help us stay in a place of dignity within ourselves, because how we conduct ourselves can either nourish our being and energy supply or deplete our being and drain our energy. Acknowledging the individual and even offering them a polite word can help you and them set the ground rules for a good conversation.

Let's say after you explain your situation they are not being receptive. So you continue with your goal and nicely ask for their supervisor. You may become more assertive in the manner that you are speaking as you try to get your point across. Let's say there has not been a resolution, so you continue up the chain of command requesting your goal to be met, but still it is not happening.

At this point you have to decide whether it is worth it to continue to pursue this goal with this company. You are spending an enormous amount of energy trying to get what you want from a party that is not hearing you. Or, you can decide that this is the time to move on and find a better fit, one that is receptive to your needs but one that also understands you as the customer.

Once you have determined your course of action, you are at ease because you have made a decision regarding what is important to you. This concept of the customer service experience can be applied to many different aspects of our lives, from the relationships we have with ourselves to the relationships we have with other people. Deciding to cut ties and stop engaging in situations that do not serve us anymore is a huge milestone in walking toward the things we want in our lives to enrich our path. We spend too much time wasting energy, trying to get what we want from individuals who really are not aligned and don't think like we do. The best thing we can do for ourselves is to decide whether we want to continue spending great amounts of energy pursuing goals or situations that may not really change. Or, we can take a leap and go where there is a meeting of the minds and where we can spend that energy toward accomplishing greater goals. There still will be difficulties but we will be able to see growth.

We sometimes forget that we have the time to consider these choices before acting; such is the reflexive response. Many continue to run away every time a problem arises, hoping it will not follow them. Some individuals go about fixing the problem the same way they have always done for most of their lives. Others follow their family's footsteps and implement the same techniques. No matter what, each person just wants his or her problems fixed. At this stage, the mind is trying to fix the problem, but deep inside the individual knows that this problem is not going away and will continue to resurface until the right solution is found. This cycle will only end when we are brave enough to take the challenge of resolving the issue in an entirely different way, and in so doing find a new perspective of how to tackle the issue at hand.

Before we are ready to take such a leap, we experience inner resistance. We try to convince ourselves that the unknown is not a good idea and that those feelings of discomfort and uncertainty are a sure sign that we must abort such notions. If we decide to challenge ourselves and have the courage to continue on this new path, we will find that we need to weigh all our options. Anything worth having in life takes work, from learning a new skill to sharpening a skill we already have, and it takes time and effort. This includes the process of coming to know our best selves. If we were not brought up to understand our actions and reactions with logical thinking, this does not mean we're incapable of acquiring such insight now, wherever we are in life.

Starting is a straightforward process:

- Be resourceful.
- Ask the advice of individuals you respect.
- Read books on the subject.
- Contemplate everything you have gathered, and then make a decision that will change your life for the better.

We may not find the answers immediately or get the input that we're looking for, but by allowing ourselves to be our own teachers, we can find amazing understanding. We should only open ourselves up once we've come up with enough answers on our own, so when someone shares advice, we can begin to gauge whether we can identify with that advice right away or realize that advice is not for us at that moment in time.

If we do share our ideas and problems with our family and friends before we have figured out where we're heading, we may receive advice that will confuse us even more. They might also bring their fears and inflexibility to our world, causing us to have more doubts about our new way of looking at life. This can also compound our dissatisfaction if we expect them to know us better than we know ourselves.

Some individuals do not want to accept responsibility for their own actions and subsequently they blame others for the misery of their lives. As long as they continue to do this, they will never have a sense of self or really get to experience what they are made of.

There are some individuals who find it hard to make a decision, not because they can't, but because they would rather follow others who they think make better decisions. These individuals have trusted others with their lives for a long time. These people want to be heard but don't know how to express what their needs are and have acquired a passive-aggressive behavior pattern. This behavior allows them the illusion that they can have some kind of control over their lives.

Every time others are in charge of our lives, we suffer immensely, because we are unable to live the life we want to live. What upsets us is the inability to trust ourselves in making the right decision, not the advice we received based on someone else's life experience. Some people may be afraid to make the wrong decision, to commit to something unfamiliar, and this fear clouds their judgment.

Whether we make the right decision or not, it is *ours* to make. With every decision, there will be challenges and successes. With both challenges and successes, we experience a shift in our lives. It might take a little while to get it right, but when we do, we will feel a sense of satisfaction that could only have been achieved through personal faith and having confidence within ourselves.

Making a choice to live a positive rewarding life takes time as well as planning and adjusting our behavior to how we see ourselves and the world around us. The more we trust our gut instincts and use our minds to help us make a decision, we will make better choices in our future.

Finding out if the relationship we have with ourselves is true to us or a combination of our family's behavior, our environment, and whoever we have allowed into our psyche, can be a lifelong journey.

Preliminary Questions

1. **Do you like who you are and who you are becoming?**
   - *If yes, write down 3 things you like about yourself.*
   - *If not, write down 3 things you wish to change.*

2. **Have you decided who you want to be?**
   - *If yes, write down what you have decided.*
   - *If not, write down what's keeping you from deciding.*

3. **Have you chosen to treat yourself with respect and love?**
   - *If yes, write down 3 ways you are honoring that choice.*

- *If not, write 3 reasons why you haven't.*

4. Are you a product of your past and feel shameful about it?

- *If yes, do you have individuals in your sphere who want to control your environment while you fall victim to their tactics?*
- *If not, write down3 examples of how you protect yourself.*

5. Do you always seek to be your best self?

- *If yes, write down 3 examples of how you continue to excel.*
- *If not, write down 3 examples of why you feel it is not worth it for you.*

6. Rather than measuring yourself against others, do you measure your growth from your past self to your present self?

- *If yes, write down 3 examples of how you feel you have grown.*
- *If not, write down 3 reasons why you feel a need to measure yourself against others.*

7. Do you allow others to mistreat you?

- *If yes, are you mistreating others as a consequence? Write down 3 examples of how you allow others to mistreat you and 3 examples of how you mistreat others.*
- *If not, write down 3 examples of what mistreatment means to you.*

8. Have you chosen to allow yourself to be flexible in life?

- *If yes, how have your conscious efforts helped you deal with different aspects of your life? Write down 3 examples.*
- *If not, write down 3 examples of the reasons why you are not flexible.*

9. Have you identified the thoughts and beliefs that no longer serve you?

- *If yes, write down 3 examples of those thoughts and beliefs that no longer serve you.*
- *If not, write down what it will take to identify them.*

10. Imagine if you could go back in time and see that child that was once you.

- *What 3 words of encouragement would you say to your younger self?*

11. Do you find that unless you are in control, everything around you is going to fall apart?
- *If yes, write down 3 things that stress you out about being in control.*
- *If not, write down 3 things you can do to let go of control.*

12. If you haven't been much of a giver, can you begin to share more of yourself in ways that would set you free?
- *Write down 3 things you would be comfortable sharing with others.*

13. Are you afraid of failure?
- *If yes, write down why and what is the worst thing that could happen if you failed.*

Emotions Simplified: Definitions and Questions

Accepted: *Consent to receive. Regard favorably or with approval.*
Do you accept who you are and where you come from?
- If yes, write down 3 traits you enjoy about your personality and 3 traits you wish to add as you grow.
- If not, write down 3 reasons you don't accept yourself.

Rejected: *Lack of acceptance.*
Do you feel rejected?
- If yes, write down 3 reasons why.
Do you want to change?
- If yes, write down 3 things you can do to change how you feel about yourself today.
- If not, write down 3 reasons that you feel that change will make no difference in your life.

Honesty: *The quality of being honest.*
Are you honest with yourself?
- If yes, write down 3 examples of what you feel you are honest with yourself about.
- If not, write down 3 examples of why you are not honest with yourself.

Deceive: *To delude oneself. Believing something is true, when in reality it is the opposite.*
Are you aware of how you deceive yourself?

- If yes, write down 3 examples of how it benefits you.
- If not, write down 3 examples of how it hinders you.

Confidence: *The feeling or belief that one can rely on someone or something: firm trust, the state of being certain about the truth of something.*
Do you believe in yourself first and foremost?
- If yes, write down 3 examples of what makes you confident.
- If not, write down 3 examples of the reasons why you don't believe in yourself.

Uncertain: *Not able to rely on someone or something, unsure about someone or something.*
Are you unsure about your character?
- If yes, write down 3 examples that make you uncertain about yourself.

Clarity: *The quality of being easy to see or hear, sharpness of image or sound, being certain or definite, having transparency or purity.*
Do you have clarity in your present endeavors?
- If yes, write down 3 examples.
- If not, write down 3 examples of why you are not clear.

Confusion: *Lack of understanding, feeling confused, and being unclear in one's mind about someone or something.*
Do you feel impatient or anxious when you are unclear of your actions? How does this affect your actions?
- Write down 3examples.
How does confusion affect how you treat others?
- Write down 3 examples.

Nurture: *The process of caring for and encouraging the growth or development of someone or something.*
Do you nurture your personal growth?
- If yes, write down 3 examples of how you nurture your personal growth.
- If not, write down 3 examples of why you don't nurture yourself.

Neglect: *Fail to care for properly, not paying proper attention to, disregard.*

Do you emotionally neglect yourself?
- If yes, write down 3 examples.
- If not, write down 3 examples of how you avoid neglecting yourself.

Do these examples include buying material gifts?
- If yes, do you really feel they fill that void?

Honor: *Great respect, adhere to what is morally right.*

Do you feel positive about who you are and the things that you are doing?
- If yes, write down 3 examples of how you honor yourself.
- If not, write down 3 examples of why you don't feel positive about yourself.

Worthless: *Having no real value or use.*

Do you feel you have no value?
- If yes, write down 3 examples of things that make you feel worthless or how others make you feel.
- If not, write down 3 aspects of yourself that you know are valuable to you that nobody knows.

Pride: *A feeling of deep pleasure or satisfaction derived from one's own achievements.*

Do you feel proud of yourself and how you are living your life?
- If yes, write down 3 examples of aspects of your life that bring you immense satisfaction.
- If not, write down 3 examples of why you don't feel proud.

Guilt: *A feeling of responsibility or remorse for some offense.*

Do you feel a sense of guilt in your life?
- If yes, write down 3 examples of things you feel ashamed about.
- Write down 3 ways you can change.

Love: *An intense feeling of deep affection.*

Do you realize that you deserve to be loved?
- If yes, write down 3 examples of what you love about your character and write down 3 more of how you can grow to love yourself more.
- If not, write down 3 examples of why you feel you don't deserve to be loved.

Hate: *Feelings of intense, passionate dislike for yourself, someone, or something.*
Do you hate the choices you have made?

- If yes, write down 3 examples of how you can change those aspects of your life.

How much do they affect your daily life?

- Write down 3 examples

Protect: *To keep someone or something from harm.*
Do you consciously protect yourself from harm?

- If yes, write down what you feel you do to protect yourself.
- If not, write down 3 examples of why you fail to protect yourself.

Endanger: *Expose to harm, put yourself at risk.*
Do you find that you are putting yourself at risk in certain situations?

- If yes, write down 3 examples of ways you have put yourself in danger.

Forgive: *The intentional and voluntary process by which a victim undergoes a change in feelings and attitude regarding an offense, the letting go of negative emotions such as vengefulness with an increased ability to wish the offender well.*
Have you forgiven yourself for things you have done in the past?

- If yes, can you list 3 examples?
- If not, write 3 reasons why you find it hard to do so.

Blame: *The act of holding responsible and/or making negative statements about an individual, indicating that his or her actions are socially or morally irresponsible; consciously or unconsciously making judgments about other people and focusing on their flaws.*
Do you blame others for what is happening in your life?

- If yes, write down 3 examples.
- Write down 3 ways you could change this pattern.
- If not, what choices have you made?

The Self Scale

On a scale of zero to ten, write a number next to each term in the left column that represents how you feel about yourself today (zero means *does not represent at all*, and ten means *perfectly represents*). Write the difference between ten and that number next to that word's opposite in the right column. For example, if you give yourself a four for **Accepted**, then give yourself a six for **Rejected**. The total across each line should equal ten.

Accepted	**Rejected**
Honest with self	**Deceive**
Confidence	**Uncertain**
Clarity	**Confusion**
Nurture	**Neglect**
Honor	**Worthless**
Pride	**Guilt**
Love	**Hate**
Protect	**Endanger**
Forgive	**Blame**

Once you have done this, add the numbers in the left column, and add the numbers in the right column. This will help you see the general balance of positive and negative perceptions that are operating in your life. The scale will help you see where your strengths are and where there's room for growth. These represent areas in your life to be aware of and work to improve.

A different way of thinking has to be administered in small doses, Otherwise, there is a chance to overdose...

GLENDA D. QUINTO

Part 2 -Family

From the moment we are born, if we are fortunate, our parents will provide us with all the necessities we need to survive. Whether they are our biological or adopted family, they can only share with us what they know. The ideal for every child is to inherit a loving family who accepts us for who we are, even when they might not agree with our decisions. In this idyllic setting, our families share patience, love, and understanding with us, and even before we are able to speak, we can perceive their tender vibrations.

As time passes, they assure us every step of the way, while ensuring our safety in times of uncertainty. Throughout childhood, they acknowledge and validate our decisions. In moments when we make a mistake, they are able to recognize the importance of trial and error as we grow. During these periods, they cultivate compassion and firmness. They realize that there is a fine line between teaching us what we need to learn with love and kindness to survive in this world and letting us know that the world can be a hostile environment and that not everyone will accept us with love and kindness all the time once we are on our own.

The importance of accountability is ingrained in this type of family dynamic. The babies are loved and nourished. As they grow and become children, they enjoy the dependability the family provides, giving them a safety net to fall back on. While they continue their journey to the teenage years, they will be testing their abilities not only with themselves but also with everyone else, especially their parents. The parents or guardians will be able to continue showing their steady but strong guidance, but the teenagers now sometimes show them rebellious acts of liberation. At this junction is where the parent will show the adolescent his or her way. It is up to the teenager to decide whether to accept his or her parent's guidance and the path that he or she has been shown, or whether to break free and embark on another path.

Parents can begin to see the fruit of their hard work as their child matures and becomes an adult. Nevertheless, if the adolescent doesn't follow their path, parents hope that the child will be strong enough to stand up for his or her own beliefs and pursuit of happiness, whatever that may be, and make a positive impact on humankind. With this in mind, adolescents will feel respected and always protected by their family, no matter what, carrying with them the core values given to them in the formative years. We must remember that our parents were adolescents once, who grew into adulthood carrying *their* parents' and also their ancestors' beliefs. They may have agreed or disagreed or, even worse, remained in conflict with what their parents considered was right for them.

Some of us were not fortunate as children to be blessed with the kinds of parents described above. And when people who experienced difficult childhoods become parents themselves, they can, unfortunately, pass on their feelings of despair and frustration. In their minds, they hoped that "you" would come into this world and help them eliminate their personal feelings of sadness and insignificance just with your presence. Many of them had little clarity and trust in themselves before you were born. They were looking for answers, and when they could not find any, they found a partner who could help them forget their past and perhaps adopted much of that person's lifestyle and beliefs. They may have ignored all the red flags that kept showing up and plunged into the relationship without a second thought. When they notice that the red flags are not going away and the feelings of sadness and insignificance have returned, they have to deal with not only their own emotions but also those of the partner they have chosen to have a child with. Now they have you, their own flesh and blood, in front of them, and all they want is for you to fill the void they so desperately feel. Everything comes back to whether they were able to know themselves well before you came along.

If you have parents who are themselves struggling, their restlessness and bitterness are vibrations you feel more often than love. It is entirely possible for a parent to realize his or her actions and the feelings that those actions create in the home. Hopefully with this realization, that parent will be able to become selfless in the task of raising a child. But awareness is key. Some parents are great pretenders, showing smiles and a peaceful countenance to all, but deep down there is discord, and their children can feel it, even when their parents are in denial.

As we get older, we inherit all these feelings, and so we begin to treat people poorly or disregard them just like we saw our parents do. Along with experiencing some confusion, we will never know true honesty, as it will be something we never genuinely experienced. When looking for praise, we will be given condemnation instead. Unbeknownst to us, we will attract people with the same feelings that we have deep inside. Some of us will become closed and distant; others will become overachievers, just trying to feel that they are good enough.

There are many avenues the human psyche takes, depending on the type of relationship one is seeking. Many will become "enablers," trying to rectify a past deed. Others will become "takers" just because that is what they were brought up to know. Either way, it is up to us to decide whether we accept this life and what it has given us so far, or if we want to take a leap of faith and choose our own path, where we are neither a victim nor an oppressor. Extremes like these are signs of powerlessness, as the person is not aware of himself or herself and is unable to acknowledge such behavior and begin to heal.

Some Advice for Negative Family Situations

Take time, be aware, and understand that you are in a difficult relationship with your family and that you wish to experience a better association. The more in tune you are with yourself and what you want in life, the easier the signs will be for you to recognize about how to make the necessary changes to create the space and life you want. You may feel that you cannot be in the same space with certain family members and also that you cannot distance yourself from them as they are your family, and with that connection comes some responsibility.

However, you can create boundaries that are healthy for you, even if others do not agree with you. There is a difference between boundaries and selfishness, and only when you are in tune and in balance with yourself will you be able to know the difference. The scales and questions are here to help you understand your choices and how you can manage your life in a better way.

In the long run, you will be happier for creating such boundaries that will allow you to be at peace and also be present with your family members, for whatever amount of time you are comfortable with, and yet remove yourself from them when you need to. Remember, this is your life, and the happiness of your being is imperative for your growth as well as for the benefit of all those around you.

If you choose not to create boundaries or become aware of your uncomfortable feelings, not only will you begin to hate every moment you are in a situation you don't want to be in, but you will also become confused as to how you treat others. Before long, you will become a difficult human being who feels unhappy in this world—all because you couldn't decipher what was bothering you, because you were choosing to be surrounded by guilt and shame, or because you were being controlled by others. One of the biggest decisions you can make in your life is whether you will stop the negative cycle that makes you unhappy most of the time and choose to create a new, happy existence for yourself and become an inspiration to others who can see that your courage to grow was more important than continuing in a situation that was futile.

Your family—father and mother, siblings, grandparents, uncles, aunts, cousins, or any other relative you call family—can only teach you what they know. We are all evolving beings, and your family might feel insulted or sad about how you want to expand or change the patterns of your upbringing. But remember, these are patterns that have been built upon as families evolve. Some are good patterns, some not so good. You always have the choice to keep the good things your family taught you and leave behind everything that does not serve you in your present-day environment.

It takes self-awareness for an individual to recognize that the type of family they come from is not necessarily conducive to a happy life or one of fulfillment. So when reading through the types of families, see if you recognize yours and whether you enjoy what they have shared with you and wish to expand on their teachings or you want to change your patterns and align yourself with one that resonates more with how you want to live your life from today on.

Types of Family Relationships: Which ones Best Describe Yours?

- A **supportive** family allows you to be everything you wish to be and supports you every step of the way while teaching you how to navigate through your life.
- An **abusive** family insults your choices and ideals while engaging you constantly in a hostile way.
- A **giving** family encourages your growth so you can succeed. Whether they themselves receive it or not, they are happy to sacrifice for the purpose of you having a better life than they did.
- A family of **takers** is there to remind you that they gave you life and everything you do belongs to them, and they feel they have a right to tell you how your life is going to be.
- A **challenging** family is constantly challenging your abilities. In their minds they feel they are helping you grow by testing your limits.
- A **spiritual** family tries to teach you the importance of staying connected to your spiritual side, rather than focusing on the material world.
- A **physical** family is an active family, teaching you to take in this world through your senses.
- An **intellectual** family teaches you to depend on your mental faculties to guide you in this life.
- An **embarrassing** family makes you feel awkward or self-conscious.
- An **overbearing** family believes that being arrogant and ruthless is the only way to succeed.
- A **monotonous** family believes in doing the same thing over and over again without changing anything in their lives.

- An **uninformed** family lacks awareness or understanding of the facts of life and can be fearful and mistrusting.
- A **simple** family believes in living an ordinary life, uncomplicated, and straightforward in nature. They are humble and unpretentious.
- An **inspiring** family believes in the importance of leading by example and creativity and consequently inspires those around them to be the best they can be.
- A **loving** family believes that as long as they show love, everything is possible.
- An **aggressive** family believes in being forceful in their actions; they believe this is the only way to be.
- A **jealous** family is always measuring themselves against other's achievements and feeling envy, rather than being the best they can be.
- A **self-conscious** family feels uncomfortable in their own skin; they are uncertain and anxious about their lives.
- An **enabling** family doesn't allow for the truth to be exposed. They can live in a state of denial, because the actualities of the facts are too much to handle.
- A **nurturing** family believes in encouraging your growth and development.
- A **holistic** family understands and believes that we are multifaceted and everything is interconnected; therefore, we are constantly adjusting our behavior and our needs according to what we need at that moment in time.

Preliminary Questions

1. Do you feel your family supports you?
- *If yes, write down 3 things you most appreciate about their support.*
- *If not, write how you feel when they don't support you.*

2. Do you come from an abusive family?
- *If yes, write down 3 ways this behavior has affected you and how you deal with others.*

3. Do you feel your family has sacrificed a lot for you to have the things

you have?

- *If yes, write down 3 examples of how their giving nature has shaped you.*
- *If not, write down 3 examples of how you think your life might have been different if they had.*

4. Is your family always challenging you to be the best?

- *If yes, write down 3 examples of how this has helped you or hindered you.*
- *If not, write down 3 areas in which you wish they would challenge you.*

5. Do you enjoy being brought up to believe in something bigger than yourself?

- *If yes, write down 3 examples of how this has grounded you.*
- *If not, write down 3 examples of what your beliefs are.*

6. Is your family overbearing?

- *If yes, write down 3 examples of how it has affected you.*

7. Do you feel inspired by your family?

- *If yes, write down 3 examples of how you are inspired.*
- *If not, write down 3 examples of how you wish they had inspired you.*

8. Have you inherited your family's self-conscious beliefs?

- *If yes, write down 3 examples of how they are influencing you in your daily life.*
- *If not, write down 3 examples of your effort to remove this traits.*

9. Is your family nurturing?

- *If yes, write down 3 examples of how their loving nature has helped you to be more giving.*
- *If not, write down 3 examples of how the lack of nurturing care in your upbringing has affected you.*

10. Have you become a jealous individual as a consequence of your upbringing?

- *If yes, write down 3 traits you have that you wish you could change.*

Emotions Simplified: Definitions and Questions

Supported: *When individuals or groups provide knowledge, experience, emotional, social, or practical help and encouragement to each other.*
Do you feel supported by your family members?
- If yes, which ones?
- If not, does their support matter to you now?

Judged: *To form an opinion or conclusion, carefully weighing the evidence in front of us.*
Do your family members judge you?
- If yes, write down 3 examples.

Acknowledged: *To accept or admit the existence of truth.*
Does your family acknowledge your way of life?
- If yes, write down 3 examples that make you realize they do.
- If not, write down 3 examples of how it would make a difference in your life.

Disregarded: *Pay no attention to, disregarding something or someone.*
Do you feel disregarded by your family?
- If yes, write down 3 examples of how it makes you feel.

Respected: *Admired deeply for someone's abilities, qualities, or achievements.*
Does your family admire the person you have become?
- If yes, write down 3 examples of how their respect makes you feel.
- If not, write down 3 examples of how you wish they admired you.

Manipulated: *Skillfull or artful management. The state or fact of being manipulated— To feel controlled by a person or a situation cleverly, unfairly, or unscrupulously.*
If your family is manipulating you, are you aware of it?
- If yes, write down 3 examples of how you feel they are manipulating you.

Safe: *Having a secure environment to flourish in.*
Do you feel your family provided a safe environment for you?
- If yes, write down 3 examples of how this helped you

flourish.

- If not, write down 3 examples of how you feel this has hindered your life.

Abandoned: *Having been deserted or cast off.*
Do you feel cast off by your family members?

- If yes, write down 3 reasons why you think they do it.

Protected: *The ability to shelter from any harm. The act of keeping someone or something safe from harm.*
Do you feel protected by your family?

- If yes, write down 3 examples of a time you felt protected by your family.
- If not, write down 3 examples of when you felt you were not protected.

Endangered: *To be exposed to harm, to be at risk.*
Is your family placing you in dangerous situations?

- If yes, write down 3 reasons why you allow it.

Generous: *The habit of giving without expecting anything in return. It can involve offering time, assets, talents, or knowledge to aid someone in need.*
Does your family offer you unconditional love?

- If yes, write down 3 specific times or ways that they have done so.
- If not, write 3 ways in which you feel that their love for you is only conditional.

Selfish: *Being concerned, sometimes excessively or exclusively, with oneself or one's own advantage, pleasure, or welfare, regardless of others.*
Are you aware when your family is being selfish?

- If yes, write down 3 things that you need to do in your own life to stop the cycle.

Dependable: *Trustworthy and reliable.*
Do you come from a dependable family?

- If yes, write down 3 areas in which you can depend on your family that you most appreciate.

- If not, write down 3 examples of how you wish to become more reliable to yourself and others.

<u>Unreliable:</u> *Not being able to rely upon.*

Can you rely on any of your family members?

- If yes, write down 3 individuals that you can depend on.
- If not, who would you like to be able to depend on and how?

<u>Trust:</u> *Reliance on integrity, strength, ability, surety of a person or thing. Confident expectations of something, hope.*

Can you trust all your family members?

- If yes, what is it about their trust that helps you when you go out into the world?
- If not, how does not having trust affect you on a daily basis?

<u>Distrust:</u> *The feeling that someone or something cannot be relied on. Doubt the honesty or reliability of, regard with suspicion.*

Did you grow up with distrust in your family?

- If yes, write down 3 examples of how it has affected you.

<u>Praised:</u> *Express warm approval or admiration of. Express one's gratitude toward someone.*

Do you feel admired by your family?

- If yes, write down 3 examples of what your family says about you.
- If not, write down 3 examples of what you could share with them about you that is admirable.

<u>Criticized:</u> *Indicate the faults of someone or something in a disapproving way.*

Does your family criticize you often?

- If yes, write down 3 examples that hurt you the most.

<u>Affectionate:</u> *Having great affection or love for someone or something; showing affection.*

In what ways does your family show you affection?

- If yes, write down 3 examples.
- If not, write down 3 ways in which you wish they would show you affection.

<u>Indifferent:</u> *Having no particular interest or sympathy; without interest or concern for*

someone or something.
Do you feel that your family has no interest in your life?

- If yes, write down 3 reasons why you feel this way.

The Family Scale

On a scale of zero to ten, write a number next to each term in the left column that represents how you feel about your family today (zero means *does not represent at all,* and ten means *perfectly represents*). Write the difference between ten and that number next to that word's opposite in the right column. For example, if you give yourself a four for Supported, then give yourself a six for Judged. The total across each line should equal ten.

Supported	**Judged**
Acknowledged	**Disregarded**
Respected	**Manipulated**
Safe	**Abandoned**
Protected	**Endangered**
Generous	**Selfish**
Dependable	**Unreliable**
Trust	**Distrust**
Praised	**Criticized**
Affectionionate	**Indifferent**

Once you have done this, add the numbers in the left column together, and add the numbers in the right column together. This will help you see the general balance of positive and negative perceptions that are operating in your life. The scale will help you see where your strengths are and where there's room for growth. These represent areas in your life to be aware of and work to improve.

Wisdom comes in all shapes and sizes,
at any age, from anyone.
Once you believe that all wisdom comes from one source,
You have stopped growing...

GLENDA D. QUINTO

Part 3 -Friends

We may have many acquaintances and are friendly with the people we come across in our daily life; however, some individuals feel that they are lucky if they have managed to gather through their life a handful of close friends. Others feel blessed to count acquaintances and family friends as their own close friends. We are lucky if we can count our dear friends on one hand. This applies even more as we get older and our lives become complicated. However, there is nothing better than when we feel at ease with our friends. Our friends are there to listen to us when everyone else is unwilling or too busy to lend an ear. They protect us when others mistreat us, and they have an ability to share the truth without painfully hurting us. They accept us for who we are without judgment. When we are with them, we feel that we belong. No matter how long it has been since we physically saw them, our connection to them is timeless. Whether we speak with them every day or once a year, it always feels right.

The selfless act of a friendship brings understanding and trust, which allows for boundless amounts of fun and joy. As time passes, we continue to build unforgettable memories that we play in our minds in times of need, to remind ourselves how lucky we are. We enjoy these friendships because they allow us to be ourselves as well as encourage us to grow in a comfortable environment.

Friends come in all different forms, including relatives you've known all your life and strangers you suddenly connect with. A stranger can provide as much insight as any relative if you know yourself well enough to allow them into your life and if you both feel the kindred spirit that has brought you together.

By nature, we are social beings looking to engage with others with whom we feel we have things in common. Sometimes we call people "friends" who we only speak with at work, see at the cash register of a store we frequent, play on a sports team with, or know as the friend of a friend. Whether the connection is deep or superficial, all are different examples of friendship. In the end, your choices and needs determine what friends you will have in your life.

Every friend we have shares with us something about them we enjoy. What types of friends we are going to attract depends on how in tune we are with ourselves.

Types of Friendships: Which One(s) Best Describe Yours?

The **childhood friend** knows your strengths and weaknesses. They are familiar with your upbringing and understand your family dynamic. You may not always agree with how they see the world, but because your friendship has lasted for so long and means so much to you, you are happy to agree to disagree on certain aspects of life. If you want to keep this friendship going, remember how much time you have invested through the years. When difficult conversations come up, you need to decide whether making your point is more important than how that point will affect your friendship in the future.

The **recreational friend** is someone with whom we share common hobbies or activities. There may not be too much depth to this type of friendship, but there is plenty of respect and camaraderie in what both individuals bring to the table. Something to remember about this friendship is that it often involves friendly competition. This competition, rather than come between you, can help you challenge each other beyond your comfort zones to achieve a lot more than you would have alone or with another individual. When your friend is more successful than you at any activity, remember that it is not always about who wins but rather who played their best game that day.

Acquaintances represent an array of friends. These include family friends, neighbors, and individuals we often see but do not engage with on a deeper level. We may not know a lot about them or them about us. However, our short interactions can be meaningful or unimportant depending on what we are looking for.

Codependent friends can be draining. If you grew up with a codependent family, it is likely that you will choose to have codependent friends. These individuals seek your attention exclusively in every way. They become jealous when you want to spend time with others. Unless you give them what they want, they will begin to manipulate you by questioning your choices and trying to plant seeds of doubt in your mind. Some of these individuals may have stronger-than-friendship feelings for you and will act upon these feelings every chance they get. They will try to sabotage your other friendships or relationships to gain your attention. If you do not wish to attract friends with these characteristics, the first step is to recognize their traits. Some of these traits are familiar to you, as you probably grew up with family members that exhibit these characteristics. Good friendships do not have conditions, only respect for one another.

Social friends are those we enjoy through an organization or some kind of group event. These include places of worship, book clubs, wine clubs, or any social events, such as concerts, games, competitions, or festivities that include a group of people with common interests. Again, the level of depth that you wish to share with them depends on you and whether you see potential for a stronger bond.

Professional friendships are mainly on one level. These individuals come together to share their professional expertise. Whether they are acquainted in the workplace, in a collaborative setting, or through work-related events, these individuals have a certain amount of respect for each other's views. Something to be aware of is that when either individual's ego takes over the domain, an uncomfortable rift can happen that can be difficult to solve. Before long, both individuals create shields around themselves, and a matter that could have been resolved in a much easier way is now a big deal. All this happens due to poor communication. Either party can at any time take the initiative to find out what is bothering the other and clear the air. This can be done by each person writing down one to three reasons why he or she is unable to come to a meeting of the minds and then share it with the other person. This is not always easy, especially in our society. But the only way to evolve and continue growing is sometimes having the courage to take a leap of faith.

Freeloader friends take advantage of other people's generosity. They attract into their realm individuals who are givers and expect nothing in return. These individuals have chosen to be takers. They may have been taught to share by their parents or teachers but have never mastered the art of sharing with others; instead they wait for someone who has poor boundaries and takes advantage of their generosity. You may do them a favor by disallowing their behavior in your presence by setting boundaries that you feel comfortable with, and they may actually respect you.

Anything is possible, especially if they were taught in their upbringing to share. These types of individuals seem to have an "it's all about me" mentality. Their prime concern in their friendship with you is what you can do for them. Now and then, if you pull away, they are not going to want to give away a good thing and will subsequently give you a small token of appreciation just to keep you on the hook. If you feel a certain type of individual is taking more than you feel comfortable with giving, test the friendship by asking for favors and things that mean something to you, and see if they come through.

Many people cannot differentiate between true friends and acquaintances, preferring quantity to quality. These individuals attract more of a superficial level of friendship, focusing on lifestyle and wealth that in their eyes will bring them better rewards and experiences. If you befriend people like this, they will sense your need to belong. Your eagerness will be obvious to them, even if you don't realize it yourself, mainly because they know you are not one of them. They will be forceful and demanding in what they want from you, and when you truly need them, they will not be available or care about your needs.

There will be peer pressure on their part as they make you jump through hoops just to see how far you are willing to go. In the end, it is all a game to them. They demand and take from you and leave you with nothing, still an outsider.

This can be a dangerous game; they know you will do anything to be accepted. In some cases, they know you will take the blame for things that were not your idea or your doing. If you had stopped to think for a moment, you would have made a better choice, if only you knew who you truly were before embarking on a need for desperate acceptance.

There are those who, from the moment you meet them, want to be your very best friend. They want to be there in your times of need or when you make a mistake. Little by little, you find yourself sharing more and more about your personal life, but they rarely share any of their life experiences with you. These friends will show up over and over again, waiting for the right time to ask you for anything they need and expect you to deliver. They believe that they have been your loyal confidante when others were not and presume you will come through for them. Though not in so many words, their attitude says, "I was there for you when you needed me," and, "I know so much about you; you don't want to piss me off."

The latter is an extreme, but it does happen at every social level. You will unfortunately have no choice but to adhere to their needs, whether you want to or not. These friends are holding you hostage, and now you find yourself agreeing to things you would have never been part of in the past—all because you didn't know yourself well enough to attract friends that you could have trusted and that could have helped you in the long run.

A **holistic** friendship encompasses everything that is good about friends, a mutual give-and-take from both individuals, with synergy running through the friendship. When both friends cherish the other's characteristics, this type of friendship can last a lifetime. Even when they disagree, these friends are able to fix their problems rather quickly and continue to enjoy their friendship.

Some Advice on Friendships Changing

From a very young age, we create bonds with friends that come and go throughout our lives. As we get older and begin to make foundations, we attract friends with similar interests. Whether those friends come from our neighborhood, school, church, recreational activities, extended family, or other family connections, we begin early on to understand what it is like to have friends and how to build a relationship with them.

Some friends remain in our lives for a long period of time as we continue to grow and share experiences together. Other times, even when we are enjoying our friendships, they fade away due to relocations, work schedules, family time, or any of the demands of daily life that can come between us and our friends.

In some cases, we may have had a strong bond with a friend, but as time passes, that bond fades away and friction begins to show up. Unless both individuals are good communicators and are able to express how they are feeling about a certain aspect of the friendship, their friendship is likely to fall apart. When a problem arises, individuals already know how much they value that specific friendship and how much effort they are willing to invest to fix the issue so they can continue to maintain the friendship. Despite every effort made from one individual and not the other, some friendships may not survive, because one or both individuals have grown in different ways. But it doesn't mean we have to dislike that individual. Instead, we can come to understand that everything has a cycle, and for every end, there is a new beginning. Accepting and allowing these changes and new thinking will help us attract friends that we are more in tune with as we continue in our journey.

Preliminary Questions

1. Write down who your friends are and the category they fall in.
Categories: ·
> *Childhood*
> *Recreational*
> *Acquaintance*
> *Emotional*
> *Social*
> *Professional*
> *Freeloader*
> *Holistic*

2. Write down three examples of your friendships that you enjoy the most.

- *What do you appreciate the most about these friends?*
- *Write down 3 examples of things your friends do that you dislike.*

3. Are you able to be honest with all your friends?

- *If yes, write down 3 examples.*
- *If not, what do you want to tell certain friends?*

4. Do you feel used by your friends?

- *If yes, write down 3 examples of the things that bother you the most about them.*

5. Have you been able to fix any issues or problems that you have had with certain friends?

- *If yes, write down 3 examples.*
- *If not, write down 3 examples of problems that you think need fixing in certain friendships.*

6. *Are there any friendships that you wish to remove from your life?*

- *If yes, write down 3 individuals you wish to remove from your life.*

7. Are there any friendships that you'd like to strengthen?

- *If yes, write down 3 individuals you want to strengthen your relationship with.*

8. Is there a certain type of friendship that you'd like to seek out?

- *If yes, write down 3 examples of the types of friendships you wish to attract into your life.*

9. Have you lost meaningful friendships in the past that you wish you could get back?

- *If yes, write down 3 things you feel are important to do to get back those friendships.*

10. Have you taken certain friendships for granted before?

- *If yes, write down 3 things you can do to change that.*
- *If not, write down 3 things you would miss about them if you lost their*

friendship.

Emotions Simplified: Definitions and Questions

Dependable: *Trustworthy and reliable.*
Do you have friends you can depend on?
- If yes, write down 3 friends you can rely on.

Unreliable: *Not being able to rely upon.*
Do you have unreliable friends?
- Write down 3 friends you can't rely on.

Attentive: *Attending to the comfort or wishes of others.*
Do your friends pay attention to your needs?
- If yes, write down 3 examples of how your friends are attentive.

Dismissive*: Feeling or showing that something is unworthy of consideration.*
Are your friends dismissive of you?
- If yes, write down their names and what they do that is dismissive to you.

Joyful: *Feeling, expressing, or causing great pleasure and happiness.*
Do your friends bring you joy?
- If yes, write down 3 examples of how your friends bring happiness into your life.

Down: *From higher to a lower position.*
Do your friends bring you down?
- If yes, write down 3 examples of their actions.

Included: *Being considered, being part of the whole.*
Do you feel included in your group of friends?
- If yes, write down 3 examples that remind you of their inclusion.

Excluded: *Deny access to someone, alienate, or consider them.*
Do you feel excluded from your group?

- If yes, write down 3 examples of how it makes you feel.

Expectation: *Strong belief that something will happen or someone will or should achieve something.*
Can you expect your friends to come through for you when you need them?

- If yes, write down 3 things that you expect from your friends.

Doubt: *A feeling of uncertainty or lack of conviction.*
Are you doubtful of your friends' true intentions?

- If yes, write down 3 examples.

Easy: *Achieve without effort; presenting few difficulties.*
Do you have effortless relationships with your friends?

- If yes, write down 3 ways in which your friendships are easy.

Challenging: *Needing much effort or skill to accomplish. Testing one's ability, endurance. Stimulating.*
Do you have friends that challenge you?

- If yes, write down 3 examples of how those challenges are affecting you, whether with growth or with confrontation.

Satisfaction: *Fulfillment of one's wishes, expectations.*
Are you satisfied with the friendships you have?

- If yes, write down 3 examples.

Resentment: *Feel bitterness or indignation toward someone.*
Do you feel resentment towards some of your friends?

- If yes, write down 3 examples.

Admired: *Regard with respect or warm approval.*
Do your friends admire you?

- If yes, write down 3 things that you think they admire the most.

Ridiculed: *The subjection of someone or something to mockery or derision.*
Do you feel your friends ridicule you?

- If yes, write down 3 examples of what they do.

Considerate: *Careful not to cause inconvenience or hurt to others.*
Do you find your friends to be considerate in your time of need?

- If yes, write down 3 examples.

Thoughtless: *A person not showing consideration for the needs of other people.*
Are your friends thoughtless in your time of need?

- If yes, write down 3 examples.

Adventurous: *Willing to take risks or to try out new methods or ideas.*
Are your friends adventurous?

- If yes, write down 3 examples of what you enjoy about this trait.

Dull: *Lacking interest or ideas.*
Do your friends stimulate you?

- If not, write down 3 examples of what you wish to change about this.

The Friends Scale

On a scale of zero to ten, write a number next to each term in the left column that represents how you feel about your friends today (zero means *does not represent at all,* and ten means *perfectly represents*). Write the difference between ten and that number next to that word's opposite in the right column. For example, if you give yourself a four for Dependable, then give yourself a six for Unreliable. The total across each line should equal ten. Refer to the list above the scale for definitions of each of these terms.

Dependable	**Unreliable**
Attentive	**Dismissive**
Joyful	**Down**
Included	**Excluded**
Expectation	**Doubt**
Easy	**Challenging**
Satisfaction	**Resentment**
Admired	**Ridiculed**
Considerate	**Thoughtless**
Adventurous	**Dull**

Once you have done this, add the numbers in the left column together, and add the numbers in the right column together. This will help you see the general balance of positive and negative perceptions that are operating in your life. The scale will help you see where your strengths are and where there's room for growth. These represent areas in your life to be aware of and to work to improve.

We are not here to compare ourselves to others,
but rather live an original existence...

GLENDA D. QUINTO

Part 4 - Love Partner

Physical attraction, as well as similar upbringings, interests, and ideologies, are the very things that we respond to when choosing a love partner. Through the process of sorting through the contenders, our brains begin a checklist of things that we are looking for in a mate and traits that we are not comfortable with. Once we have chosen (and are chosen by) that special someone to be our lifelong companion, we feel a sense of belonging and comfort that allows us to open up, hopefully with great honesty, which will bring about fulfillment and emotional safety that no other relationship can imitate. That person provides a sort of grounding for us that allows us to let go and feel free to be who we want to be by being real in the relationship. The best relationships are those in which both individuals feel this way and can therefore grow together.

In a healthy love relationship, we do not have to think constantly about the condition the relationship is in. This allows us to spend more time pursuing our gifts, our professions, or the tasks that need our attention. When we achieve this, we feel so good that we want to be better in every way, live longer, take care of our bodies, and become nicer to everyone, not just those who we need to be nice to. The sun seems to shine wherever we go, and no matter what life throws at us, it does not matter: we are in love.

Furthermore, even when we hear difficult news or face a struggle, for the mere reason that we are in a good place, we are able to handle the situation much better than we would have if we had not felt so loved.

When a relationship is going smoothly, it only takes 10 percent of our attention. When there are more problems than solutions, then it takes 90 percent of our attention and then some. One of the most important things we need to do is to be real and honest with ourselves about the relationship. Consciously or unconsciously, we know whether or not we are in the relationship for the right reasons or not.

Some Advice on Clarifying the Relationship

If you are not sure where the relationship is going, be frank with yourself and your partner. Have fun if that is what you are looking for, but make your intentions known to your partner. Clarity in your intentions will help you be more assertive in your decisions and direction. By sharing this with your partner, you will have more room for communication and development expansion and less confusion. There will be times when what you want does not work for the other partner. You always have choices if your partner means enough to you. You can adjust your needs without compromising your integrity, but never to a point where there is a chance you may lose yourself.

Knowing yourself will help you gauge how far you are willing to go to gain agreement. Allowing others to steer you puts you in a place of confusion, and it can leave you feeling fearful and uncertain. There is always room for growth, if that is what you are seeking. Just make sure that there is always a give-and-take—as long as it is what you both want it to be. It takes maturity and understanding to follow such thoughts and ideals. The longer we practice, the better we get at it and the happier we will be, as well as those we are involved with.

The longer we play games, the longer we remain in the past. Having a second agenda can get us into trouble. Some may find that they gave up on love due to painful breakups or by seeing parents' marriages fall apart. When this happens we aren't being true to ourselves. We may be in a relationship for a week or for years without really connecting. In these situations, both partners involved will generally know there is something vital missing, like real intimacy, acknowledgment, or understanding of what true love really represents.

One of the most important aspects in a relationship is the ability for partners to communicate in a way in which both understand what the other is saying. Even if both partners speak the same language, the way they go about communicating their wants and needs can be so different that they might as well be speaking a different language. Here partners can feel frustrated and hopeless. This is a time to really dig deep and have a one-on-one with that person you fell in love with and come to an understanding that even though there is love, how you both go about expressing and acknowledging the needs in the relationship are contrary to what the other needs.

Instead of becoming a more evolved you, one that is free to be the individual you want to be within yourself and the relationship as the years go by; you actually chip away slowly your sense of self and before long you can't recognize the person you see in the mirror or the person you wanted to be when you entered the relationship. This also fractures the relationship as a whole, when both partners feel it but can't seem to figure out a way to fix it.

Some people continue to stay together, mainly because they have forgotten what true love feels like, or they never saw it in their parents and can't really recognize it, or they were once in love, but from lack of maturity, they let it slip away. There are some who will stay in a bad relationship or a marriage because they are too afraid to leave or because of the children. Some have an affair because they don't know how to be honest about their problems and keep seeking answers somewhere else. They hope that someone else will come and help them forget their reality or save them from a situation they got themselves into, placing a Band-Aid on their hearts.

There are some who know their partners have been unfaithful but continue to stay with them. These people are unable to have synergy in their lives due to the fact that their minds and hearts are always in conflict. They know if this person has done it once, they will do it again; it is in their nature. The individual who is being disloyal is also trying to run away from their problems, aligning themselves with other individuals who have the same type of mind-set. Since these people are also confused, rather than dealing with their problems, they continue to have clandestine affairs.

Some people get to a place where they are so tired of the betrayal and lies that all they want is comfort, even if this means settling for someone uninteresting that provides certain benefits, such as protection or social status. If you fall into this category, be aware that the partner you "settle" for will give you the same treatment you give him or her, as like attracts like. They will mislead you in ways you mislead them. They will be distant and unexciting, waiting for you to make a move, just like you are expecting.

When we aren't being fulfilled by the romantic relationship in our lives, sometimes we begin to act out by finding fulfillment with materialistic objects. Enjoying life's comforts is part of being human. But the comforts of life cannot fill our feelings of emptiness. No matter how much we indulge, we will never find what we are seeking. Overeating, drinking, and shopping among other things are signs of unhappiness. We stay in a state of denial by forgetting our true self, and again, little by little, we chip away at any small identity we ever had, until we do not recognize ourselves anymore but rather a person who gave up on themselves and their dreams.

You owe it to yourself to have the best relationship you can have, and while you are in a dysfunctional one, you are not able to heal yourself and find the confidence within to make the right choices.

Types of Love Relationships: Which One(s) Best Describe Yours?

There are many types of love-partner relationships; love is different for everyone. Some basic ones are business, family, love, lust, friendship, and holistic.

Some individuals have a **business** love-partner relationship, which is more like a partnership. These individuals feel that each of them must bring certain attributes and contributions to the relationship for them to remain on a path of growth, which ultimately they feel is going to bring happiness and prosperity.

When first meeting such individuals, they are more inclined to ask impersonal questions that can sound more like a job interview than a courtship. "What are your short-term goals?" "What are your long-term goals, as far as your work and 401k?" "Do you own or rent?" "What did you major in?" Although these individuals are attracted to each other in the first place, they feel a need to ask the above questions first before asking deeper questions about the individual's personal life, like thoughts and wishes. "What are your hobbies?" "What's your favorite food?" "What makes you smile?" "What are you looking for in life?"

These types of people want their assets to match with the other partner's so they can feel that they are an equal in the relationship and not either inferior or being taken advantage of. They may also be the types to be extremely organized, scheduled, and busy. This type of thinking allows them a sense of control over their lives, leaving little room for error.

If this describes you, some questions you might ask yourself are as follows:

- Am I growing under this controlled environment?
- Am I flexible enough to accept my partner for who he or she is?
- Am I keeping everything in order so I can have more time to explore and grow in a deeper way?
- Am I allowing my partner to share with me things I didn't know before about him or her?
- I may be challenging myself at work, but am I challenging myself in the relationship? Am I learning to deal with situations in the relationship differently than I would have done before?
- Do I trust my partner enough to share with him or her not just my basic day but what truly bothers me or what matters to me?
- Do I find myself being dishonest because no matter what I say, I am going to be criticized or judged?

In an era where social media and cyber communications have become the norm, many people have accepted a more detached and aloof way of life. While we are transmitting our thoughts through this medium, none of our traditional senses—sight, smell, taste, hearing, and touch—are present. Above all, we are sentient beings who need our traditional senses to have more of a fulfilling experience, regardless of how we decide to approach a relationship. Both individuals need to be on the same page and feel comfortable in this scenario. Some may be willing to consider the idea that there are other facets of the relationship worth exploring.

A love-partner **family** relationship is one of the more complicated ones. Some people come together who feel the reason for their existence is more about procreation and the ability to provide for their family until death do they part. This does not mean there is little love between them. However, their intimate relationship is secondary to the importance of the whole family. These people choose to get married, have children, and follow some if not all of their family's footsteps. They are not so much concerned about the evolving of self but rather do their growing through life's forceful changes and through their children. Again, as long as both parties feel the same way or at least want similar experiences, they will be able to thrive. In this love-partner family relationship, just like in any other, it is always important to address what is meaningful for you and what is meaningful to your partner. This will benefit your relationship. And a little flexibility will provide your children with new tools and ways to handle future problems and challenges.

The scales provide you with words that allow you to really gauge how you are feeling. You can sit with your partner and open the channels of conversation if you are both willing to make the effort to listen to what else is important in your life and whether you feel it is worth it to evolve and grow in a different way.

In a love-partner **love** relationship, both individuals want first and foremost to be loved for who they are. Being in love carries with it tremendous feelings of happiness and contentment. No matter what is happening in your life at the time, those feelings of love will keep you strong and going in ways that nothing else can. Although you believe that person is your world and the reason why you feel so amazing is because of the way they love you, actually the deepest feelings of love come because you have allowed that individual in. Your sense of who you are and what you want is what has allowed you to open a part of you that is allowing you to feel love for yourself, empathy, trust, and understanding, in ways that under any other circumstances you would not. When you both feel the same type of intensity for each other, you both do whatever it takes to keep those feelings alive.

A ***treasure box*** is a metaphor for a box where partners can sit down and write all the things that matter to both of them, including: what each one needs and wants in the relationship, the things that will break the relationship, how much you allow your friends or family to dictate your life, your perfect way to spend the weekend. You can also use the questions in this book to get know each other more, whether you like to travel, stay at home, watch movies. The questions do not have to be deep necessarily, but you can ask questions about subjects that matter to you. By taking the time to examine all these questions and actions, it will help you both to realize that to continue feeling in love, you both have to hold the treasure box and cherish it.

This relationship is always giving and taking just enough to make sure your partner's feelings are taken into consideration. Whenever these couples confront any situation, they accept the obstacles and challenges as a unit, always relying on each other, and never allowing a third party to come between them. Subsequently these couples end up evolving and becoming better people. This type of understanding allows them to continue to protect their love, not only because it means so much to them, but also because it is the key to their happiness.

Just like in any other type of relationship, when one or both individuals begin to take the relationship for granted, problems begin to arise. The signs can be scattered and faint, but they are signs that things are changing. Perhaps you used to look at each other in a certain way and don't anymore. Maybe you start forgetting to call when you said you would. Maybe your partner used to really hear what you meant when you said something, and now he or she doesn't. Maybe you're becoming less respectful of each other's time. Your partner might still be affectionate like he or she used to be but doesn't remember what's important for you.

Everyone's life evolves one way or another as circumstances and environments change. The question is, even though the above changes are happening, can you address them and still feel heard? A sense of doubt can enter the relationship when you or your partner forgets what it is about the relationship that made you so happy. If you are aware of your relationship and of yourself, you can address the issues right away before they become real obstacles. Otherwise, by the time you figure out what is happening, the other individual's feelings might be too far away for you to get them back.

A love-partner **lust** relationship is based mostly upon physical attraction. This attraction can be so strong, you might feel as if you are soul mates. Regardless of what type of relationship you have, physical attraction has to be present for the relationship to survive. If all you have is lust and little to nothing else in common, eventually you may find yourself at a loss in this relationship. However, if your feelings are strong for that person, you will challenge yourself to want to be more, to look within and find some answers about yourself you never thought about. If you are both mature in your thinking, you have the ability to take the relationship to many levels. Again, this can only happen if you both feel the same way about each other.

A love-partner **friendship** relationship is based on trust and commonalities. These couples care about each other as friends first. Their priorities are to the friendship first. There is a mutual respect that allows them to be who they want to be and at the same time blossom in an environment they feel comfortable in. As mentioned, this couple started as friends, enjoying each other's company. At the beginning, they knew what to expect from each other. For the most part, but not always, these individuals' feelings have progressed into a deep, fulfilling relationship. They already are able to communicate freely, and now they have chosen to explore the many other facets of their lives on a different level.

One of the things to bear in mind in this type of relationship is that both individuals probably know a lot about each other and now everything becomes more personal and has more meaning. There is a kind of accountability that didn't exist while they were just friends. For example, one or both partners might forget to share certain things with the other—things that were not really important when they were friends but are now important in the relationship.

For example, one partner goes and buys a high priced item, such as a new television or a car, or goes to the mall on a shopping spree without mentioning it to their partner, then the partner sees the items at home. Or the one partner fails to tell their partner that this Friday they are going away with their friends for the weekend, and the other partner doesn't find out until they see them packing a bag. Or that they lost their job, but the partner doesn't find out until they see their partner lounging at home on a work day. Or that their mother is moving in, without consulting them. Or that they brought a pet home.

When they were just friends, the timing of events was not important, but now that they are in a relationship, these situations can come across as one partner taking the other one for granted because they used to be "just friends." They feel so relaxed with you that they do not need to try. If such observations are not taken into consideration, there is a chance that you could lose not only your relationship but also your best friend.

A love-partner **holistic** relationship is arguably the best type of relationship to have, as it embodies all the other types of relationships into one. If you find yourself able to balance all the facets of your love relationship according to what you are looking for in your life, then you will have found the perfect harmony. Every relationship needs some love, friendship, lust, family, and business structure to stand the test of time. By allocating what is important to both of you in the order that is most beneficial, you will have the ability to thrive, dream, and grow within your love-partner relationship. There is a certain kind of wisdom and maturity required to achieve this relationship. When both partners are able to communicate freely to the point where they can agree to disagree in particular areas of the relationship and still understand and respect each other's perspectives, these holistic couples will be able to have a meeting of the minds, hearts, and souls. They realize that to continue to share these feelings of being in love, both partners must hold that treasure box closely, and in doing so they will always be truthful and respectful of each other's needs and wants.

Things to be aware of in a relationship:
- Always remember to stay connected to each other, even if you are far away. Let it be known what that person means to you.
- Whatever you both did at the beginning of the relationship, you must continue to do, as these are the reasons why you both fell in love with each other.
- Even if you have children, change jobs, have personal or family losses, or you both have difficulties, you must be able to remain a unit that is able to communicate your wishes and fears to each other. Nobody outside your relationship knows you both better than the two of you.
- If you or both of you allow any kind of disrespecting actions or disregarded feelings to happen in the relationship without addressing them, you will lose the precious gift you once had.

Only you know whether your relationship is staying alive and happy or whether it has begun to wither away. There are many clues along the way that allow you to either address the problems you are seeing and fix them or ignore them as they continue to pile up right before your eyes. The choice is always yours in whether this relationship means enough to you to fix what's broken.

Now you have to decide whether to remain in a relationship that you already feel and know is not what you thought and hoped it was going to be, or decide if it would be best to leave it before it turns into something you do not recognize, or to stay in the relationship, knowing that your heart's desires will not be met. By staying in a relationship that does not give you what you need, you run the risk of lowering your self-esteem and your confidence. You also may not be sharing your best with your partner. Are you giving as much as you are receiving? Does your partner feel the same way? Or are you both deceiving yourselves by pretending that either it's not happening or that somehow it is going to get better?

As you are unable to fix your relationship, you begin to concentrate on other areas of your life as a distraction. You also begin to criticize and manipulate other people in your life, because suddenly you have no control in your own relationship. By accepting what your relationship has become, you may realize that you do want that person in your life but not anymore as the love-partner relationship you once had. This desire to continue the now-unfulfilling relationship might exist because you have many commitments together; you like the other aspects of your life together, or you may have children together. Either way, it is important to accept what your relationship has now become.

At such a point as this, however, you should ask yourself: how much am I willing to sacrifice of my inner self for all the other benefits that I'm getting? Consider some of the signs of a relationship that's on the rocks.

Signs that you may be sacrificing too much of your inner self:

- You are unable to have restful sleep, as you know a big part of you is not real anymore and you are not doing anything proactive to change it.
- You find yourself putting on or losing weight because your subconscious mind is preoccupied with anxiety and you are either eating too much or starving yourself to match your emotions.
- Instead of having glowing energy and a happy demeanor, you look tired and are feeling emotionally very low.

- You get sick more often and your immune system is compromised.
- You become less trusting and more skeptical of others.

There are times when we scream and fight, literally or figuratively, because we care enough about something that we're afraid we're going to lose. When it means so much to us that the idea of losing it frightens us to the core, we sometimes lash out. Once we realize that what we are trying to do is control and steer the outcome of an event, we can also recognize that truly the only control we have is how we react to it.

Pushing and trying to get others to see things our way is like driving a car on a highway and trying to get every driver around us to drive like we do. All we really can do is be an example or share without expectation, whether we agree with our partner's decision or not. The true decision lies within us to decide whether we are willing to compromise because that specific situation is worth compromising or whether such a situation is a deal breaker for us.

This does not mean you give up what you feel strongly about; what it means is that the person you are sharing your thoughts and ideals with doesn't share the same ideals. For example, the two of you want to listen to a different radio station. One is not better than the other, just different. You have three choices: One, you can compromise and choose to listen to your partner's station, as well as for them to listen to yours. You may not always enjoy it, but you can find appreciation in sharing something different with your partner that you may not have known before and viceversa. Two, you can just listen to your station without a second thought about what your partner may want. Three, you can can find someone who listens to the same station you do. This metaphor works well with many other life situations, it all depends on what you want in life.

There are some people who like challenging relationships in their lives, because the challenge helps them grow. Others do not want to be challenged or tested but instead want to be the person who guides the relationship. Others want to be guided. They are not comfortable making decisions, and they would rather someone else make the decisions for them. They are willing to compromise in areas that allow them to be free in other areas. And there are some who want to share the responsibility of being guided when the other knows best and guiding when they know best. In this situation, both partners have to be confident enough with themselves and with their roles in the relationship for them to feel comfortable.

Signs that you are losing that loving feeling.

- Once you had a strong physical attraction, and now you do not feel that same chemistry.
- Before, you could have sex any time, anyplace, anywhere, with or without alcohol or any other kind of stimulant. But now you find that you need to be inebriated to even get in the mood.
- You feel that the only way now that you will sleep with them is if your partner buys you a gift or takes you out so you can be in the mood.
- You used to bring them coffee in the morning and now you don't.
- You used to call them and see if they needed anything from the store.
- You used to surprise them with gestures of love.
- You always used to be kind and gentle with your words and actions.
- You would offer a hug or a shoulder to lean on.
- You would kindly listen to their issues and try to help them.
- You would listen to what they had to say even though they didn't want help in fixing the issues, but rather they just wanted someone they cared about to hear them.
- You would share a joke or a funny fact.
- You would go for walks together.
- You would never go to bed upset.
- You would make time to be together.
- You would go dancing, or go to the movies, or have a romantic dinner, or goof around the way you used to when you were young.
- When your partner begins to pay attention to others more than you, and you begin to wonder if he or she has moved on.

If you find yourself craving that desire you once had for your love partner and you look for it with someone else, before you know it, you have put yourself in a difficult situation where you are having an affair with someone outside your relationship just to feel those amazing feelings you once had, and all because you did not have the courage or the confidence to communicate to your partner the things that are important to you. By not communicating and breaking the trust in your relationship, you are also ignoring your core existence by shortchanging yourself and giving yourself the opportunity to be loved in your entirety.

People will treat you the way you allow them to treat you. In the end, whether you are deceiving your partner or yourself, this becomes an emotional game that ultimately hurts you and devalues who you are.

Preliminary Questions

1. Is your partner willing to hear what you have to say, genuinely?

- *If yes, write down 3 examples of what this means to you.*
- *If not, write down 3 examples of what it would feel like to be heard by your partner.*

2. Are you able to speak your mind and yet come to a happy resolution?

- *If yes, write down 3 examples of what you do to make this happen.*
- *If not, and you feel that you are pushing your ideas against your partner's wishes—write down 3 examples of how you feel you could change this.*

3. Can you deny and ignore what you believe to be true in your heart?

- *If yes, write down 3 reasons why.*
- *If not, what do you need to do to be true to yourself?*

4. Do you like who you are in this relationship?

- *If yes, write down 3 examples of how it has changed you for the better.*
- *If not, write down 3 examples of how the relationship has changed you.*

5. Is there room for growth?

- *If yes, write down 3 things you wish to implement.*
- *If not, write down 3 reasons why you feel there is no need for growth in the relationship anymore.*

6. Are you in a relationship with someone who understands your thinking and shares the same ideals?

- *If yes, write down 3 choices you made to attract this relationship?*
- *If not, write down 3 reasons why you are in this relationship.*

7. Are you growing from each other's experiences and having a meaningful life together, or do you feel that there is a constant battle?

- *Write down 3 examples of each.*

8. What can you share with your partner that will give him or her some insight into who you are?

- *Write down 3 examples.*

9. Do you feel you understand your partner and your partner understands you?

- *If yes, write down 3 things your partner needs from you.*
- *If not, write down 3 things you need from your partner for the relationship to thrive.*

10. Do you think more or feel more in this relationship?

- *Write down 3 things you think about the relationship.*
- *Write down 3 things you feel about the relationship.*

11. Do you respect your partner enough to tell the truth?

- *If yes, what 3 things would you tell him or her that would allow you to feel free in this relationship?*
- *If not, write 3 reasons why you are afraid to be honest*

12. Do you stand by your own decisions even when confronted by your love partner trying to sway you against your choices

- *If yes, write down 3 things you do to stand by your decisions and feel good about the outcome.*
- *If not, write down 3 things you can do to stand by your decisions and feel good about them.*

13. Do you allow your friends or relatives to sway you when you know deep inside what the right thing for you to do is?

- *If yes, write down 3 examples of how you think this affects your choices.*

Emotions Simplified: Definitions and Questions

Cherished: _To protect and care for someone lovingly._
Do you feel loved and protected by your partner?
- If yes, write down 3 examples of what he or she does to make you feel loved.
- If not, write down 3 reasons why you don't feel loved.

Insignificant: _Too small or unimportant to be worth consideration._
Do you feel insignificant in your relationship?
- If yes, write down 3 examples of situations where you feel insignificant in your relationship.

Free: _Not under the control or in the power of another._
Are you free to be who you want to be in your relationship?
- If yes, write down 3 examples of what it means to you to feel free.
- If not, write down 3 reasons why you do not feel free.

Controlled: _The power to influence or direct people's behavior or course of events._
Do you feel controlled in your relationship?
- If yes, write down 3 examples where being controlled is detrimental to your relationship.

Fulfilled: _Bring to completion or reality. Achieve or realize._
Do you feel fulfilled in your relationship?
- If yes, write down 3 examples of how you achieve this.
- If not, write down 3 reasons why you are not in a fulfilling relationship.

Unfulfilled: _Not having fully used or exploited one's abilities or character._
Do you feel unfulfilled in your relationship?
- If yes, write down 3 reasons why you are still in it.
- If not, provide 3 positive examples.

Heard: _To be listened to, given or paid attention to._
Does your partner hear you?

- If yes, write down 3 examples of how this makes your relationship better.
- If not, write down 3 examples of how it makes you feel.

Ignored: *Refuse to take notice or acknowledge.*
Does your partner ignore you?
- If yes, write down 3 reasons why you allow it.

Complete: *Having all the necessary or appropriate parts.*
Do you feel completed in your relationship?
- If yes write down 3 examples of how it completes you.
- If not, why have you chosen to stay?

Incomplete: *Not having all the necessary or appropriate parts.*
Do you feel incomplete in your relationship?
- If yes, write down why you feel incomplete.

In love: *An intense feeling of deep affection.*
Do you feel that you are in love with your partner?
- If yes, write down 3 examples of what makes you feel in love.
- If not, write down 3 reasons why you are in the relationship.

Indifferent: *Having no particular interest or sympathy, unconcerned.*
Are you in an uninspired relationship?
- If yes, write down 3 examples of why.

Honest: *Free of deceit and untruthfulness, sincere.*
Do you feel you are in an honest relationship?
- If yes, write down 3 examples of what makes your relationship honest.

Dishonest: *Behaving or prone to behave in an untrustworthy or fraudulent way.*
Are you in a dishonest relationship?
- If yes, write down 3 examples of what makes your relationship dishonest.

Desired: *A strong feeling of wanting to have something or wishing for something to happen.*

Do you feel desired by your love partner?

- If yes, write down 3 examples of the importance of this in your relationship.
- If not, write down 3 examples of why you don't feel desired.

Unexciting: *Not interesting or stimulating.*
Does it bother you that you are in an unexciting relationship?

- If yes, write down 3 examples why.

Validated: *Demonstrate or support the truth or value of something.*
Do you feel validated in your relationship?

- If yes, write down 3 examples of how your partner validates you.
- If not, write down 3 examples of how you wish you were validated.

Rejected: *Dismiss as inadequate, inappropriate, or not to one's taste.*
Does your partner reject you?

- If yes, write down 3 examples of how your partner rejects you.

Secure: *Feeling safe, stable, and free from fear or anxiety.*
Does your partner offer you stability?

- If yes, write down 3 examples of how your partner makes you feel secure.
- If not, write down how you wish your partner would make you feel secure.

Insecure: *Subject to fears and doubt.*
Does your partner make you feel insecure?

- If yes, write down 3 examples of what your partner does to make you feel insecure.

The Love-Partner Scale

On a scale of zero to ten, write a number next to each term in the left column that represents how you feel about your love-partner relationship today (zero being *does not represent at all,* and ten being *perfectly represents*). Write the difference between ten and that number next to that word's opposite in the right column. For example, if you give yourself a four for Cherished, then give yourself a six for Insignificant. The total across each line should equal ten.

Cherished	**Insignificant**
Free	**Controlled**
Fulfilled	**Unfulfilled**
Heard	**Ignored**
Complete	**Incomplete**
In love	**Indifferent**
Honest	**Dishonest**
Desired	**Unexciting**
Validated	**Rejected**
Secure	**Insecure**

Once you have done this, add the numbers in the left column together, and add the numbers in the right column together. This will help you see the general balance of positive and negative perceptions that are operating in your life. The scale will help you see where your strengths are and where there's room for growth. These represent areas in your life to be aware of and to work to improve.

Some may have more experiences than others in certain realms,
But none of us have all the answers.
We are all just drops in this ocean, but together we can find the
answers...

GLENDA D. QUINTO

Part 5 - Work

S ome people receive all the support and love that they need to follow their dreams and contribute to mankind from their relatives and teachers. Some may not be as lucky to receive that type of encouragement to succeed. However, it is in those times of doubt when our instincts urge us to pursue our desires regardless of how difficult our circumstances may be. In the end, no matter what adversities come our way, there are individuals out there that have a burning desire to succeed and will work and work until they achieve their goals. They may not take home the gold medal or get paid millions of dollars to do it, but their own sense of accomplishing their innate desires and goals makes them winners in their minds and consequently they become happier individuals.

When we are in that perfect space of understanding our calling and what the path entails, we find ourselves making the right decisions. This trust allows our instincts to guide us while we keep honing our craft, or our abilities to do a task and do it well, regardless of what it is. Eventually, we will see the fruits of our labor, the ability to make a living from our talents. This does not mean that there is less effort involved, but rather, there is a synergy between our mind and soul. This helps us better commit to finishing the task at hand and helps us feel a sense of fulfillment and significance that we can only find while pursuing our purpose.

As the saying goes, "If you love what you do, you will never work a day in your life." To truly love what we do, we have to recognize that our career passion might require sacrifices. People who devote many hours to their ideas at times must sacrifice enjoying life's comforts as well as time with family and friends. This type of dedication allows the creative mind to explore and expand in ways we would have never been able to unless we gave our minds the chance to see beyond our daily thoughts. We are always thinking and planning our ideas, spending hours upon hours devising the best way to put together what we see in our minds and then finding a way to share it with the world, hoping to make a difference.

The wonderful part about this type of calling is that the payoff comes with extraordinary rewards. These rewards are not always of a monetary nature, but they can carry a strong sense of personal accomplishment.

Looking back

To be able to get more insight into your current situation, sometimes it is good to look back into the history of how you arrived here. Looking back, are you able to remember what compelled you to follow this profession in the first place? When was that deciding moment when you said to yourself, *"This is what I want to do for the rest of my life." "This is what I want to practice and I want to do it so well, and be so proficient at it, that as the years pass, I will become an expert in my field."*

Do you remember receiving all the support you needed from those you care about? Do you remember being so enthusiastic about your decision that they not only felt it was right for you but they also offered you total support? Had anyone in your family chosen to follow the field you were embarking into, or were you the first one? Were your decisions based on what was expected of you as part of a family legacy, a profession that has been passed down from generation to generation?

All these decisions began to shape your life. Either way, once the decision was made, your next step was to get the training you needed to secure success. This could have included, going to college and making sure your grades remained at a constant high, or making sure you would get into the graduate school you wanted. Once there, the pressure continued, never letting go of the importance of keeping your grades and character in good standing. The load only became more evident, once you realized that to get into the organization you wanted to get into, you must also have work experience in that specific field.

Every step you took mattered. Every decision was carefully weighed as you drew closer to your dream job. When others were enjoying the evenings and weekends, you were putting in the hours, either studying or working hard towards your dream. You did whatever it took at the time to make it happen, including possibly having two or three jobs simultaneously and/or taking care of family. Nothing was left to chance. You knew in your mind that the course was set and that you were not stopping until you arrived at your final destination. All throughout your schooling, training, and work experience, you reminded yourself of the dream you had and that was your motivating factor.

Landing that job in that particular field, in that particular organization was your focus, you knew that once you were there that you had arrived. And from then on, life would be bliss, right? Well, is it? Is it everything you thought it was going to be? Was all your hard work and sacrifice worth it?

Now that you are here, new questions and challenges have entered your realm in ways you never actually considered or thought about before. Such as, is the job itself everything you hoped it would be? As you go about your day, do you feel that you are able to use every experience and skill you have learned in the past to help you advance in your career? How do you find your work environment? Is it what you thought it would be?

Now that you are in this place, is the company the type of organization you thought it would be? Do they deal with the company's internal issues in a professional, beneficial manner that you are proud of? Do you think the company represents themselves in an honest, professional way? Do these things matter to you? Is the company's morale high or low? Do you think it stems from the people in charge? Is your work environment hostile or friendly?

So here you are now, after all the work and training you did, you find yourself either exactly where you want to be or questioning the decisions you made long ago. Are you questioning your decisions, and feeling frustrated and defeated because of the amount of work and time you put into something that hasn't materialized the way you thought it was going to be? If that is the case, can you bring yourself back to the drawing board and begin to break down your choices? Or, are things going very well with your work life?

If you love your profession but not the environment you work in, can you begin to search for companies that you admire in your field? What is it about those companies you love the most? Are your skills and your work experience enough to land yourself a job there? Or do you feel you need to come up with a better plan before putting yourself out in the market again? Can that plan include a different approach to how you have handled a situation in the past?

Breaking down all the aspects of your work into manageable sections can help you see things differently. I have included questions to be viewed from entirely different points of view.

- What is the skill you bring?
- How is this skill received by your company?
- What is your interaction with executives and your boss?
- What is your interaction with your co-workers, peers, and subordinates?
- Do you have interaction with vendors and suppliers?
- Do you have interaction with customers and clients?
- How much do you enjoy being at work?
- Do you want to be promoted, and is this an option at your company?
- How much training have you received, and do you want more?
- How much training do they offer?
- Do you feel that they respect you?
- Do you respect the company as a whole?
- How much do you enjoy the actual work that you do?
- Is your compensation satisfactory?
- Do you feel you have a good benefit package?

- How much free time do you get to spend pursuing other interests, or time with family?
- Are you geographically where you want to be?
- If you travel for work, do you want to travel more or less?
- Can you see yourself retiring with this company?

Breaking down everything into small parts as shown above can help you see what exactly is it about your work that you love and can live with, and what no longer is making you happy. As you can see, there are many factors and dynamics to your profession. Weighing positive versus negative interactions, tasks, and overall contentment is what will help you determine whether you are going to stay and make the adjustments you need to succeed, or whether it is time to go and find something that resonates with you on a deeper level.

Every job or career has the ability to offer something more than compensation in exchange for your skills. Depending on what we want out of it is how we are going to decide how to prioritize our choices. Some of these choices can be broken down depending on how they make us feel and what objective we are going to have. For example if your main objective is to feel a sense of **achievement**, your aim is trying to personally feel accomplished in the work place by making sure the job is done successfully through your efforts and skills. You are hoping that by doing this job well done, that it will bring you a feeling of respect from your peers and co-workers, subordinates or employees and hopefully recognition amongst the executives of the company, your supervisors, and also that you will be highly regarded by your customers and clients and others with admiration for the way you achieved the goal and that in your field of work you will be recognized.

If your objective is to feel a sense of **contribution**, your mission is to implement your skills and be part of something that will bring about a result of helping or contributing to the betterment of another or others in the bigger picture. You may not need to feel a sense of achievement necessarily. As long as you feel you have contributed to the advancement of the goal, this will create a sense of happiness and contentment for you and it will show the executives, supervisors, and peers and co-workers that you are ready to do your part and be respected in your field.

If your objective is to feel a sense of ***significance***, your key purpose is to make sure everyone around you knows your worth and what you bring to the table. You want the executives of the company to see you as an important asset to the company, for your supervisors to know that your talents and skills bring sufficient benefits to the company, for your peers and co-workers to notice your work and share it with others in your field of work. You want your vendors and suppliers, customers and clients to realize and regard you as the person who makes all this happen.

If your objective is to feel a sense of ***discovery,*** you will always be searching for new ways to do something different or better than before or pushing the boundaries of your comfort zone by challenging yourself in ways others may not do. You enjoy sharing your findings with your peers and co-workers. The approval of your supervisor hopefully will allow them to see that you are someone who can present a different way to look at things. The company's executives will be pleased because your findings could help the advancement of the company as well as gain more of a footprint on that specific market.

If your objective is to feel a sense of ***organization***, your purpose is to make sure that the world you work in is organized in a particular way. You thrive on making sure the structure or the arrangement of the organization is handled in a professional, orderly manner, where everything has its place and everything you have control of runs like a well-oiled machine. By having this arrangement, you are confident that your supervisors will appreciate your diligent work, which you hope they will share with the company's executives. Your peers and co-workers, subordinates or employees might even benefit from your structure, which consequently it can benefit the company's customers and clients, vendors and suppliers.

If your objective is to feel a sense of ***creativity***, your quest is to use your imagination in every way possible. Whether you work alone or as part of a group, producing original ideas that can be transformed from a thought to a tangible product is what drives you. Receiving consent from your supervisors, company's executives, your clients and customers, vendors and suppliers gives you a feeling of acceptance and that your skills and talents are good enough for others to want to commission your work.

You are also hoping to become a catalyst and an inspiration to others in your realm.

If your objective is to have a sense of ***entrepreneurship***, your goal is to build a business model that requires leadership, initiative, innovation, team-building, and management abilities amongst other positive traits for the business to succeed. This high-risk venture can produce outstanding results and profits or devastating losses depending on the individual's experience and how they choose to approach not only the obstacles along the way but also the everyday running of the business. Once successful, recognition will come from those who will appreciate and benefit from such an endeavor.

If your objective is to have a sense of ***development***, your mission is to help grow a specific product, task, or concept to its fruition. Your skills and talents are sought out here, where your supervisors can rely on you for your expertise. Where your peers and co-workers, subordinates and employees know you will lead them towards accomplishing the goal and the company's executives can be sure you will make use of the best resources out there, making your contribution an asset to the company and the field you are in.

If your objective is to find a sense of ***respect***, you apply your skills and talents in a methodical manner. You conduct yourself with honor, and you follow orders, ethics, and traditions with utmost respect. Such qualities are commendable amongst the executives of the company and recognized by your supervisors and at times used as an example to share with your peers and co-workers, subordinates and employees in how to perform or adhere to certain tasks or aspects in the work place.

If your objective is to find a sense of ***accomplishment***, your skills and talents will give you the opportunity to prosper in an environment where you feel comfortable with what you are doing, and how you are helping the task advance. With your type of mindset, you are wired to execute and complete any task given to you with proficiency. Your vendors and suppliers can appreciate your diligence and good work ethic. Your sense of pride is obvious to your supervisors, who can acknowledge you by letting the executives know how well you manage a task. Your subordinates can learn from your skills and your clients and vendors will benefit from your competence and expertise.

Company Culture

Relating to some of the objectives above can help you realize where you feel your skills and talents lie and whether you are maximizing your potential where you are or whether you already have a good grip on what you are doing but where you are is not the right fit for you. A company's culture can tell us a lot about what type of individuals are running the company and what they expect, what they want and are willing to give their employees or executives.

Understanding this before fully committing yourself can help you make a better choice. Do you respect the company you are seeking to further your employment with? How much do you know about the company's principles and work ethics to feel that your contribution would not only help your advancement but that of the company's? Can you see yourself growing in that company? Are you proud to say who you work for and talk about the great things the company is doing? Can you see yourself learning from that environment and then branching out on your own, if that is your wish? Do you enjoy the hours you work? Does it allow for you to entertain other pursuits?

Can you see yourself getting ready for work and looking forward to what the day or shift will bring? Are you learning and developing in a friendly environment? Do you feel you make a difference? Or are they ignoring your thoughts and declining any skill or expertise you bring to the table? Do you get along with the individuals you work with? Do you see yourself spending time with them outside work? Geographically is the job favorable to you?

All these questions can help you decide whether you are part of that company's culture and want to continue with it or if you are ready to find a company where their culture is better suited for you. The more questions you ask yourself, the better the chances you have to fulfill your dreams. There are many reasons why we choose to leave our job. On the positive end of the spectrum, we have come to a realization that we are ready to evolve and take the next step. Everything that we have been through has brought us to this point, where we do not have fear about the future but believe that we are ready for something better. This does not mean the job we are leaving is bad, but more that we have outgrown it. What we are seeking is change so we can find more challenging tasks, self-development, and overall satisfaction in our journey.

On the negative end of the spectrum, in the workplace we may be dealing with issues that we just cannot handle any longer. Perhaps our managers, bosses, co-workers, subordinates, are incompetent at times, have a superiority complex, or engage us with constant confrontation, and no matter what we do, it is never good enough. We may also be experiencing a lack of job satisfaction, a lack of opportunities for self-development, a lack of career prospects, a lack of infrastructure within the workplace, or a lack of rewards or appreciation for going above and beyond what the work requires.

Leadership

For a new project to get off the ground, the company needs people with many different types of skills, including knowledge and the ability to organize, as well as hardworking staff in the office to keep things running smoothly. Any organization also requires the people who work behind the scenes, such as the caretakers and janitors. Without them, the environment at work would be intolerable. They deserve appreciation as much as anyone else. In a work setting, unless we have camaraderie with coworkers, accomplishing tasks can be difficult. Something as little as showing kindness to those around us can increase their self-respect and feeling of significance in this life. Whether we realize it at that moment or not, these are the small deeds that nourish our well-being.

This type of universal understanding starts with those who we work for and those who we work with. We might be lucky and have a boss who is self-assured enough to have courage and be of assistance to our coworkers and us. A good boss realizes that to achieve goals, he or she must bring out the best in everyone to succeed. This type of supportive work environment allows for everyone involved to achieve his or her personal best, whatever that might be. However, when the company or the manager fails to recognize their employee's potential, or the employee does not fit in a particular role, that employee may find him or herself being disregarded and his or her suggestions shut down.

It takes confident managers who care about their employees to figure out how to help their employees succeed under their wings. To determine what each of their employees brings to the table, managers can select the right positions for their employees according to their personal skills. These abilities might not be apparent or written in their resume; however, the manager can find out what they are by simply creating a work environment where the employees feel safe enough to open up to them. Given the chance, the employees will come up with ideas that will improve the work force as well as benefit the organization as a whole.

All these ideas can happen when managers are comfortable within their role and feel confident in the company they work for. Situations begin to break down when someone is in a position of leadership and does not feel respected or appreciated for his or her efforts. As soon as a manager starts to feel uncertain about the company, this creates a domino effect for the entire company. This can cause his or her employees' families to begin to feel the tension that Mom or Dad is bringing home from work. As emotional beings, it's hard for us to ignore the stress and even harder to stop it from affecting our loved ones.

If you find yourself in a situation where you are not heard at work, are you able to talk with your manager about what you can do to improve your situation? What ideas can you bring to the table to increase your group's work performance? Don't spend hours doing the same repetitive tasks that are without satisfaction, but rather figure out a way to increase your productivity and work toward a goal that you can reach and feel good about. It is always your decision if it is worth your precious time to stay within that specific position or even within the company.

Types of Managers: Which One(s) Best Describe Yours?

A **challenging** manager continually tests your abilities and pushes you beyond your comfort zone. A **lazy** manager is not interested in challenging, motivating, or caring about you or the company's growth. A **motivating** manager stimulates your interests and enthusiastically cheers you on. An **overbearing** manager believes that the only way to lead you is by letting you know that if you don't perform, you will be criticized and arrogantly dominated. A **caring** manager understands that to get the most out of you, he or she must truly feel concern and have interest in what you are doing. An **inexperienced** manager lacks knowledge and skills that ultimately will hinder you and the ability to grow to your full potential. An **inspiring** manager realizes that through example, creativity, and collaboration, you can accomplish great things that subsequently will reflect back on them. A **dismissive** manager ignores anything of value that you may express. He or she lacks interest and believes that you have little to offer but the basics. A **standard** manager does the job to the level of quality that is required. He or she will perform every task according to the guidelines and follow protocol in every way—nothing more, nothing less.

If you are not in your ideal job, do you have enough confidence and courage to begin searching for a position that fulfills you, a position where you feel you have something to contribute and feel appreciated? We all have choices we can make at any given time, and even though sometimes those choices are limited, we can always find a solution to our situation. When we are willing to put the time in and work diligently toward those solutions instead of spending hours thinking about how much we detest our situation, we are on the path to having figured out a way to live a better life.

There are many who choose not to place such emphasis on creating but rather on other aspects of their lives that they consider more satisfying. These people find comfort and joy with tasks that are not necessarily of a specific talent. However, their abilities and gifts offer tremendous contribution to the whole. These types of contributions give them a sense of belonging.

These people find accomplishment in everything they do. They enjoy being part of the group and succeeding by working with others to create perfection.

Preliminary Questions

1. **Are you happy with the position you have at work?**
    - *If yes, write down 3 reasons why you love your job.*
    - *If not, write down 3 ways of how you can either advance in your company or begin to look for what you want.*
2. **Do you get along with your manager and/or co-workers?**
    - *If yes, write down 3 things that are important to you about getting along with them.*

Glenda D. Quinto

- *If not, write down 3 reasons why you don't get along with them.*

3. Do you admire and understand your company's outlook?

- *If yes, write down 3 key elements that you most admire and understand.*
- *If not, write down 3 key elements that you wish to find in a company.*

4. Do you feel your company provides you with all the tools you need to succeed?

- *If yes, write down 3 examples of how the company helps you grow.*
- *If not, write down 3 examples you wish your company would provide you to help you succeed.*

5. Do you feel your skills and talents are well utilized at work?

- *If yes, write down 3 examples of how your skills are being effective.*
- *If not, write down 3 reasons why they are not utilized.*

6. Do you work in a competitive environment?

- *If yes, write down 3 examples of how that environment affects your work in a positive way.*
- *If not, write down 3 examples of how it affects you in a negative way.*

7. Do you work in a creative environment?

- *If yes, write down 3 examples of how that environment instills your creativity.*
- *If not, write down 3 ways you wish to implement more creativity into your work.*

8. Do you work in a controlled environment?

- *If yes, write down 3 factors that affect your productivity in this environment.*
- *If not, write down 3 factors that you would benefit from working in such environment.*

9. Do you find collaboration at work?

- *If yes, write down 3 examples of the benefits you receive from working as part of a team.*
- *If not, write down 3 examples of how working as a team would help you and your co-workers excel.*

10. Are you satisfied in the field you are in?

- *If yes, write down 3 features you most appreciate about the field you work in.*
- *If not, write down 3 key elements you want in the field of your choice.*

11. Are you able to communicate freely with your supervisor and/or co-workers?

- *If yes, write down 3 essential benefits you and the company receive from having open communications.*
- *If not, write down 3 reasons why you are staying in this environment.*

12. **Do you want the opportunity to grow within the company?**
    - *If yes, write down 3 key aspects you would bring to the position you are after.*
    - *If not, write down 3 reasons why it is important for you to stay where you are at.*

13. **Does your job provide you with great benefits?**
    - *If yes, write down 3 things you most appreciate about these benefits.*
    - *If not, write down 3 things you want to have in your next job opportunity.*

14. **Are you compensated adequately at work?**
    - *If yes, write down 3 things that you have done to create this. (i.e. training, experience, dedication)*
    - *If not, write down 3 things you can do to feel adequately compensated at work.*

15. **Overall, are you happy with what you bring to the table?**
    - *If yes, write down 3 characteristics that help you stand out from the rest.*
    - *If not, write down 3 characteristics you can incorporate to help you stand out from the rest*

A sense of synergy and balance is imperative for you to become successful in any field or anything you would want to accomplish in life. Below are some examples of being in harmony not only with ourselves but with those around us and beyond.

We see this unity of purpose when we watch a ball game and see the players bringing their best game on that day and competing against those who also want to excel. These people may feel that they are competing against each other, but what is actually happening is they are all competing against their best selves. There is a euphoric feeling that comes with competing among so many talented players. Their energies are being pushed beyond their normal boundaries, allowing them to thrive and see how much further they can go.

Whether it is a Little League game or watching the Major League playoffs, the feeling can be the same. Those of us watching the game or competition can vicariously experience a similar emotion through those who are propelling themselves to be the best. We enjoy rooting for their teams, and although we are not playing the actual game, we feel part of the team. Some of the spectators might play the game as a hobby on a smaller scale and look for inspiration from those who have made it their career. The young ones watch their every move and learn, seeing themselves as professionals one day.

Another example: There are those who ponder science and space research. They are seekers of a different kind, but their feelings of exhilaration and passion to seek beyond are the same as those who physically exert themselves. Those who have made a commitment to search for answers find solace and achievement in supporting what was once a thought with actual facts and data. With every discovery there is excitement and opportunity for growth. There is something about science that is unpredictable yet thrilling, especially when a mistake turns into triumph. All of a sudden the dam has broken, filling not only the originator but also the community of seekers with new answers and inspiration. These create excitement in a virtual world where regardless of their geographical address, everyone tapped in wants to be involved.

Again, whether the findings are in a primary school setting or at a scientific laboratory with all the bells and whistles, the euphoria is the same. These individuals as a collective are experiencing unity as a whole or a subliminal connection within each one of us.

Emotions Simplified: Definitions and Questions

Accomplished: *Achieve or complete successfully.*
Do you feel accomplished in your work?
- *If yes, write down 3 examples of your work achievements..*
- *If not, write down 3 examples of what you need to do to feel accomplished.*

Disappointed: *Fail to fulfill the hopes and expectations of someone or something.*
Are you disappointed at work?
- *If yes, write down 3 examples of what bothers you the most.*

Encouraged: *Give support or confidence to someone.*
Do you feel encouraged at work?
- *If yes, write down 3 examples of how you are encouraged.*
- *If not, write down 3 examples of what type of encouragement would help you excel at work.*

Discouraged: *Cause someone to lose confidence.*
Do you feel discouraged at work?
- *If yes, write down 3 examples of how you are discouraged.*

Inspired: *Aroused, animated, or imbued with the spirit to do something.*
Are you inspired at work?
- *If yes, write down 3 meaningful examples.*
- *If not, write down 3 examples of what you think would inspire you at work.*

Deterred: *Discouraged from doing something.*
Do you feel you are deterred from tasks at work?
- *If yes, write down 3 examples of how it makes you feel.*

Optimistic: *To be hopeful and confident about the future.*
Are you optimistic about your job prospects for the company you work for?
- *If yes, write down 3 examples of where you see yourself in the company over the next 3 years.*
- *If not, write down 3 things that you can do to change your dynamic and make your future more clear.*

Pessimistic: *Tending to see the worst aspect of things or believe the worst will happen.*
Do you see a future in the company you work for?
- *If yes, write your vision.*
- *If not, write down 3 reasons why you haven't made a move.*

Included: *Contained as part of a whole being considered.*
Do you feel included at work?
- *If yes, write down 3 examples of how being included has helped you and the company flourish.*
- *If not, write down 3 examples of how not having a voice affects you at work.*

Excluded: *Denied access to a place, group, or privilege.*
Are you feeling left out at work?

- *If yes, write down 3 examples of how it affects you.*

Secure: *Not subject to threat. Feeling safe, stable, and free from fear or anxiety.*
Do you feel secure in your position at work?

- *If yes, write down 3 examples that give you such security.*
- *If not, write down 3 examples of how it is affecting your daily tasks.*

Threatened: *Hostile action against someone in retribution for something done or not done.*
Do you feel threatened at work?

- *If yes, write down 3 examples of instances where you felt threatened.*

Proud: *Feeling satisfaction as a result of one's own achievements, qualities, or possessions.*
Do you feel proud of the work you do?

- *If yes, write down 3 examples of how it fulfills you.*
- *If not, write down 3 examples of skills you have that you are proud of.*

Dismissive: *Unworthy of consideration.*
Do you feel unworthy at work?

- *If yes, write down 3 reasons why you are still there.*

Respected: *Having a good reputation especially in a field of knowledge.*
Do you feel an overall sense of respect at work?

- *If yes, write down 3 examples of what you have done proactively to gain respect at work.*
- *If not, write down 3 examples of what respect means to you.*

Criticized: *To express disapproval of someone.*
Do you feel criticized at work?

- *If yes, write down 3 examples of situations when you were criticized at work and whether you feel any of them were valid.*

Recognized: *Show official appreciation. Reward formally.*
Do you feel recognized at work?

- *If yes, write down 3 examples of what the company does to recognize you.*

- *If not, write down 3 examples of the things you do that you wish you were recognized for.*

Ignored: *Fail to consider.*
Do you feel ignored at work?
- *If yes, write down 3 examples of how the company fails to consider you.*

Appreciated: *Be grateful for something. Recognize the full worth. To admire and value something or someone. To understand the worth or importance of someone or something.*
Do you feel appreciated at work?
- *If yes, write down 3 examples of how they compensate you.*
- *If not, write down 3 examples of how you wish to be compensated.*

Overlooked: *Pass over someone in favor of another. Fail to notice.*
Do you get overlooked at work?
- *If so, write down 3 examples of when it has happened and what you did about it and 3 examples of what you can do differently next time to change the outcome.*

The Work Scale

On a scale of zero to ten, write a number next to each term in the left column that represents how you feel about yourself today (zero equals *does not represent at all*, and ten equals *perfectly represents*). Write the difference between ten and that number next to that word's opposite in the right column. For example, if you give yourself a four for accomplished then give yourself a six for disappointed. The total should equal ten. The total across each line should equal ten.

Complete this scale first for yourself and for how you feel about your actual work, and then, if applicable, complete the scale again with your supervisor in mind, and again for your coworkers or any other individuals who have a direct impact on your work life, whether positive or negative.

Accomplished	**Disappointed**
Encouraged	**Discouraged**
Inspired	**Deterred**
Optimistic	**Pessimistic**
Included	**Excluded**
Secure	**Threatened**

Proud	**Dismissive**
Respected	**Criticized**
Recognized	**Ignored**
Appreciated	**Overlooked**

Once you have done this, add the numbers in the left column together, and add the numbers in the right column together. This will help you see the general balance of positive and negative perceptions that are operating in your life. The scale will help you see where your strengths are and where there's room for growth. These represent areas in your life to be aware of and to work to improve.

Success will frighten you in the same way failure will. What is frightening is the unknown.
The day you figure out how to deal with it is the day you will know what you are made of...

GLENDA D. QUINTO

5-Part Emotional Inventory

Self.

Start to pay attention to how you feel about a difficult situation.

- What do you need to do to remove yourself from it, or can you tackle the challenge by trial and error until you get it right?
- Write down 10 things you love to do that you are not currently doing.
- Can you begin to practice just one of the things you love to do, once a week, or once a month?
- Can you make a promise to yourself to do it, just like you would make a promise to anybody else that was important to you?

Family

- Can you love and respect your family, although they may not agree with you?
- Are you able to see that they cannot understand your choices but that doesn't mean you need to prove your point?

When you are free inside, you do not need anyone's approval. You know where you are going, and that is all that matters.

Friends.

- If you have friends that really do not feel like friends but rather acquaintances, is it because you are afraid to be alone or have a need to be liked and be part of a group?
- Can you begin to see other's characteristics that you are attracted to?
- Do you feel that others are in control of your life?
- Does it affect your freedom? Can you gain control of your life?

Love partner

- Are you in a relationship that leaves you empty at the end of the day but feel you have invested too much time and effort to leave, so you live unhappily?
- Can you be truthful with yourself and decide if this is the way you want to live until the day you die?
- Have you thought that maybe your partner deep inside feels the same way but doesn't want to disturb the situation because he or she is also afraid?
- Can you have the courage to understand where you are and where you wish to be?
- What do you need to do to create happiness in your life?

Work

- Do you feel fulfilled at work? Or are you ready to make a change? What can you do today to begin making those changes? Most successful people are successful because they are doing what they want to do, and they believe in themselves, even when others were against their choices.
- Some of the choices you need to make are going to be hard, but ultimately you need to decide whether you are going to keep your world standing still or whether you are ready to see what you are made of.
- What small aspect in your life can you change today to begin this process?
- Can you practice it for the whole week and then the whole month?
- Can you have a place somewhere in your home or work where you can cut and paste your ideas, ideals, dreams, choices, and words of encouragement on a board to remind you of where you want to be?
- Can you do the exercises on the *Self, Family, Friends, Love-*

Partner, and *Work* scales so you can begin to actually see where your mind is and where there is room to grow?

Start now. Take time now to awaken your awareness to be better today than you were yesterday to yourself and your fellow men and women and see how you can change your reality just by shifting a few habits, a few perspectives, a few characteristics at a time. The trick is asking yourself these questions:

- "Did I do my best today?"
- "Can I do better tomorrow?"
- "Am I proud of myself and what I have accomplished?"

We are all equipped with certain abilities and provisions that will allow us to acquire more knowledge and understanding about the human race. There is something about you that you need to share in this world, no matter what it is. You owe it to yourself and others to share your gifts.

There are those who have come into this life with the ability to really make a change. These individuals can have the following traits or advantages:

- A natural talent or an aptitude that they were born with or were able to bring into fruition.
- An inner drive to share something with the world.
- Born into the "perfect" family.
- Substantial financial means.
- A desire to overcome difficulty against all odds.

They have the potential to decide whether they want to use their means for their own personal growth as well as the betterment of their fellow men or just for the betterment of themselves. It would be up to the individual and how they are able to see how their decisions affect their happiness and their way of life in the long run.

Our minds are free to think, and we are free to do whatever our hearts desire. Even so, the way we reject change and make choices that leave us short of our destiny's calling proves that in spite of the freedom we do have to follow our hearts. We are creatures of habit. If we take a look at our lives from an outsider's point of view, we might be left wondering why we are not rising to the challenge of making better and more conscious decisions about our personal relationships with ourselves and with humankind.

There is a lack of honor and nobility in our execution, when deep inside we know that honor and nobility exists within us, even if we were not brought up to know this. We see it in others, and we may not recognize it straight away, but somehow it makes us feel good when someone is honorable and generous with us. At that moment we can make a conscious decision to adopt those traits and apply them in our lives by paying them forward. This trait can bring, if we would only exercise it, much happiness and peace of mind. Honor and nobility would also allow us to be catalysts for good in helping the people around us to rise to the challenge of being more than they could ever imagine.

We don't have to spend money on charitable contributions in order to be charitable. Every day we have the chance to be charitable, one action at a time, from the way we treat our bodies to the way we interact with the people we come into contact with.

Our own mortality is something that many of us choose not to think about. It's almost like we believe death is the kind of thing that happens to other individuals, not us. We act as though if we ignore it, it won't come knocking, at least until we feel we're ready for it.

Food for Thought

If you knew you were going to die tomorrow, what would you do different today, if anything? Write down five examples of what you would do.

If you were able to write your own obituary, what do you wish people would have known about you? Write down five things.

If you were to see the obituary of someone who had an impact on your life, whether positive or negative, can you write down 3 things you wish you had said to them?

We are multifaceted beings who find it hard to work on ourselves a lot of the time. Instead we look for distractions as much as we can. The day always comes when someone reminds us of something or someone in our past we have chosen to forget or to deal with. At these moments, our minds and emotions call into question certain aspects of our lives, and we have to decide whether we are going to deal with the issue right there and then or continue our old patterns.

Just like in the house of our mind and soul, there will be individuals that will compel us to enter those rooms we wish could remain under a lock and key. If we could just for one moment in time be brave and take a chance to hold our breath and dive into our fears, we could see that we have created a wall so high that it stops us from getting hurt.

This fear of going back inside those rooms paralyzes us, creating pain and anguish that can manifest in many ways, including our bodies getting sick, or an inability to accomplish daily tasks or future goals we have set forth. However, if we could see past the fear and take control of our lives, instead of allowing the situation or the individual who hurt us to keep controlling our lives, we could see that we have a chance to face aspects of our lives that need our help and rescuing. These aspects that need our courage, so that little by little we can become whole again. And only we can gain back that control.

The more you sharpen your self-awareness, the better your life will be. You are in charge of your life, and the better you know yourself, the better your choices and your overall fulfillment will be. Those who have strong ties with individuals and feel they cannot break away from a situation can assess their circumstances and find out what it is about that situation that is preventing them from having a fulfilling experience.

There may be a sacrifice to make and some work on your part, but nothing can compare to the freedom that comes from being who you want to be. When all is said and done, by getting to a place of strong emotional well-being, you can serve as a positive role model to others, whether they are children, lovers, friends, or coworkers. Most of all, by putting yourself at the top of your list and doing the work that needs to be done to formulate the best version of YOU, by association you are leaving your stamp on the world for all to see.

Every time we have negative thoughts, we are putting ourselves in a place where our psyche and health feel as if they were under fire. By learning to master our emotions, we have the ability to shift those feelings from anguish, fear, anger, and doubt to *peace, trust, happiness and certainty*. These feelings can bring an extraordinary positive vibration if we allow it.

Although this might not be the case in our present reality, we can facilitate our mind by adjusting and choosing thoughts that help us to be in a state of contentment.

Just like we have five senses, these five areas in our lives are the most important, the *self, family, friends, love-partner, and work*. Managing these areas and how we prioritize them will help us on our road to happiness.

After you answer the questions posed in this book, the final and best question you can ask yourself is this: "What can I do differently next time to change the outcome of a situation?"

If something means enough to you, you will make the change when you are ready. Every time you overcome an obstacle, you allow for new experiences to enter your life. Whether those experiences are difficult or wonderful—or both—they will add character and maturity to the depths of your being.

Earthbound is what we become when we can only see this world through a microscope.
Imagine what you could see if only you took a chance…

GLENDA D. QUINTO

Conclusion

This journey is a very personal journey that begins with you and your self-acceptance, your ability to be honest with yourself at any given moment and whether you are able to embrace life's changes with confidence and clarity. You must feel proud of who you are and how you do it, and having another day to get it right, to enhance the gift that is you—to nurture your body, as your cells wait for you to give them the nutrients they need to help you thrive. Because once you do, your body will burst with energy and intention helping you think clearly and hence helping you fulfill your dreams and desires through synergy. This will help you to enhance your ability to honor and protect yourself, by loving yourself in ways you may have never known.

All these positive thoughts can help you decide little by little to begin to remove thoughts of uncertainty, unworthiness, past mistakes, self-loathing, and realize that to continue to contemplate these thoughts will allow your mind to take you to a room where there is only darkness and confusion rather than the beautiful rooms in the other parts of your house where there is light and abundance. It is up to you to turn on the light in those dark rooms and free yourself of any darkness and confusion that has followed you your entire life.

Once you begin to master how you see yourself, you can begin to see other aspects of your life in a different light. You will begin to have less expectations and more empowerment about how your family treats you or how you interact with them. You will be able to create better boundaries that at the beginning will feel alien to you but in time will feel good and ultimately will bring you a sense of happiness that you may not have experienced before.

The domino effect has begun, from seeing and treating yourself differently to how you interact with your family. Then, your friends come into play and now you have more tools and understanding about how you begin to attract exactly the type of friends you want in your life and how to remove yourself from those that are not in vibration with you any longer. Again, this is not to say they are bad people necessarily, but rather you are on different paths.

At this point, you have gained momentum and feel in control of your life and your actions, and, yes, you may stumble, but hopefully with these tools you can pick yourself back up and learn from your mistakes, giving you another chance to get it right.

Now that you are on your way, you can begin to have feelings for another in ways that are different to how you feel about yourself, your family, or friends. Hopefully you have found someone who inspires you, makes you laugh, is interested in you and what you have to say, and they have respect and admiration for your beliefs. You should feel that you are learning from them; they are bringing out the best in you and you are bringing out the best in them. And even when you may not agree, you are able to respect each other's ideals.

You will find that you love who you are in this relationship and everything that they bring as well as what you bring, but maybe at some point, things have changed and somehow you cannot get back to that place where you both truly loved and respected each other.

With all of your tools and newfound understanding of yourself and how you deal with your family and friends, you can decide that this is a time for change. Maybe in the past you have criticized and pulled the relationship into pieces and noted to yourself how that individual does not give you what you need. You could have the courage to leave the relationship or create a controlled environment where you give ultimatums for change, or otherwise you leave.

Maybe now with your awareness, you can understand that if you both are not seeing eye to eye on things, there is time to move on graciously. Now there is no need to forget what you both brought to the table but instead to be grateful to have had someone in your life that brought you so many gifts on so many levels and they have helped you to grow.

By allowing yourself to disengage in an honorable way, you allow for healthy and new experiences to come into your life. If they brought you pain, it is up to them to find out if their path is the correct path for them. As long as you continue to be affected by their actions, you are doing yourself a disservice.

You are at the epicenter of change. The ripple effect that will happen once you understand what your actions can bring and how they will affect every single aspect of your life, is that positive changes will come. By fighting change, like a small drip that never stops, it will manifest with illness and confusion. By embracing change, it can bring you happiness that you could not have ever imagined.

By finding out what you are made of, the life tapestry that you have woven so far can help you envision where your powers and gifts lie. Find out what you love to do, how you can be of service to humanity, even on the smallest of scales. You will have the chance to change someone's life, just by being kind. Or by helping someone in need, or by being courteous to everyone at your job, or by inventing something that will help humanity. There are always going to be difficulties and difficult people, but you have the choice and control, whether you choose to align yourself with such situations and individuals.

To evolve and become the person you wish to be, your desire to grow has to be as important as your desire to stay alive. If you are taking the time to read this and explore the changes you wish to make, then you owe it to yourself to use those tools to become the person you wish to be. Everyday you have a chance to grow and make a difference, only if you give yourself the chance...

The journey begins and ends with you. This book is about breaking down and simplifying how you look at your emotions, to help bring about positive changes in your life. Each of us is just one small piece of a huge energy system. We all need each other. By making these small changes, we as a whole will rise beyond our wildest expectations.

About The Author

Glenda D. Quinto was born in London and grew up in Colombia. After studying at Dover College in Kent, England, she gained extensive experience in personal growth and development. Her clinical interests include family dynamics management, drug addiction, codependency, and bipolar disorder.

Passionate about helping people unlock a deeper understanding of their own emotions, Quinto wrote *Emotions Simplified: A Practical Self-Help Workbook* as a handbook for those who wish to explore their full potential. She currently lives in Sarasota, Florida, with her family.

Acknowledgements

I would like to thank my friend Deana Anne Maggard for encouraging me to write this book, my brother Daniel for his valuable insight, my brother Jonathan for his contribution, and Aitziber Sueiro, for sharing with me significant information. I also could not have done this without the collaboration of my Managing Editor, Juliana Inhofer, of Alchemy Publishing Group, LLC, who helped me through the process of writing my first book while keeping it true to my voice. And most of all, my daughter, Fiona Rose Quinto for inspiring me every day to be the best human being I can be.